CCNP Security SENSS
Exam (300-206)

Technology Workbook

Implementing Cisco Edge Network Security Solutions (SENSS)

Associated Certification: CCNP Security

---

www.ipspecialist.net

[Document Control]

Proposal Name	:	SENSS 300-206
Document Version	:	2.0
Document Release Date	:	20 September 2019
Reference	:	CCNP_SEC_WB_SENSS

Feedback:

If you have any comments regarding the quality of this book, or otherwise alter it to suit your needs better, you can contact us by email at info@ipspecialist.net
Please make sure to include the book's title and ISBN in your message.

About IPSpecialist

IPSPECIALIST LTD. IS COMMITTED TO EXCELLENCE AND DEDICATED TO YOUR SUCCESS.

Our philosophy is to treat our customers like family. We want you to succeed, and we are willing to do anything possible to help you make it happen. We have the proof to back up our claims. We strive to accelerate billions of careers with great courses, accessibility, and affordability. We believe that continuous learning and knowledge evolution are most important things to keep re-skilling and up-skilling the world.

Planning and creating a specific goal is where IPSpecialist helps. We can create a career track that suits your visions as well as develop the competencies you need to become a professional Network Engineer. We can also assist you with the execution and evaluation of proficiency level based on the career track you choose, as they are customized to fit your specific goals.

We help you STAND OUT from the crowd through our detailed IP training content packages.

Course Features:

- *Self-Paced Learning*
    - O Learn at your own pace and in your own time
- *Covers Complete Exam Blueprint*
    - O Prep-up for the exam with confidence
- *Case Study Based Learning*
    - O Relate the content to real-life scenarios
- *Subscriptions that Suits You*
    - O Get more pay less with IPS Subscriptions
- *Career Advisory Services*
    - O Let industry experts plan your career journey
- *Virtual Labs to Test your Skills*
    - O With IPS vRacks, you can testify your exam preparations
- *Practice Questions*
    - O Practice Questions to measure your preparation standards
- *On Request Digital Certification*
    - O On request, digital certification from IPSpecialist LTD.

About the Authors:

We compiled this workbook under the supervision of multiple professional engineers. These engineers specialize in different fields, i.e., Networking, Security, Cloud, Big Data, IoT, and so forth. Each engineer develops content in its specialized field that is compiled to form a comprehensive certification guide.

About the Technical Reviewers:

Nouman Ahmed Khan

AWS-Architect, CCDE, CCIEX5 (R&S, SP, Security, DC, Wireless), CISSP, CISA, CISM is a Solution Architect working with a major telecommunication provider in Qatar. He works with enterprises, mega-projects, and service providers to help them select the best-fit technology solutions. He also works closely with a consultant to understand customer business processes and helps select an appropriate technology strategy to support business goals. He has more than fourteen years of experience working in Pakistan/Middle-East & UK. He holds a Bachelor of Engineering Degree from NED University, Pakistan, and M.Sc. in Computer Networks from the UK.

Abubakar Saeed

Abubakar Saeed has more than twenty-five years of experience in Managing, Consulting, Designing, and implementing large-scale technology projects, extensive experience heading ISP operations, solutions integration, heading Product Development, Presales, and Solution Design. Emphasizing on adhering to Project timelines and delivering as per customer expectations, he always leads the project in the right direction with his innovative ideas and excellent management.

Muhammad Yousuf

Muhammad Yousuf is a professional technical content writer. He is a Certified Ethical Hacker (v10) and Cisco Certified Network Associate in Routing and Switching, holding a Bachelor's Degree in Telecommunication Engineering from Sir Syed University of Engineering and Technology. He has both technical knowledge and industry sounding information, which he uses perfectly in his career.

Table of Contents

About this Workbook

This workbook covers all the information you need to pass the Cisco CCNP 300-206 exam. The workbook is designed to take a practical approach to learning with real-life examples and case studies:

- ➢ Covers complete SENSS 300-206 blueprint
- ➢ Summarized content
- ➢ Case Study based approach

- ➢ Ready to practice labs on UNL/VM
- ➢ 100% pass guarantee
- ➢ Mind maps

Cisco Certifications

Cisco Systems, Inc. is a global technology leader, specializing in networking and communications products and services. The company is probably best known for its business routing and switching products, which direct data, voice and video traffic across networks around the world.

Cisco offers one of the most comprehensive vendor-specific certification programs in the world. The Cisco Career Certification program begins at the Entry level, then advances to Associate, Professional and Expert levels, and (for some certifications) caps things off at the Architect level.

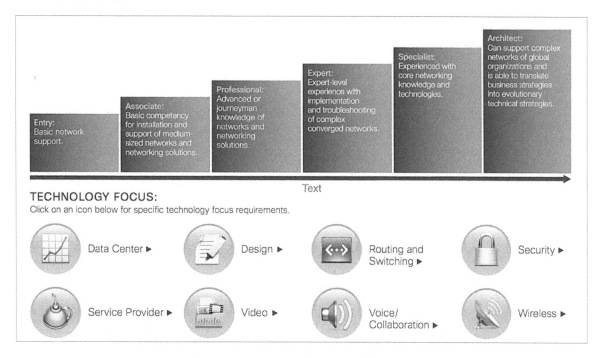

Figure 1- Cisco Certifications Skill Matrix

How do Cisco Certifications Help?

Cisco certifications are a de facto standard in networking industry, which help you boost your career in the following ways:

- ✓ Gets your foot in the door
- ✓ Screen job applicants
- ✓ Validate the technical skills of the candidate
- ✓ Ensure quality, competency, and relevancy
- ✓ Improves organization credibility and customer's loyalty
- ✓ Required to maintain organization partnership level with OEMs
- ✓ Helps in job retention and promotion
- ✓ Boosts your confidence level

Cisco Certification Tracks

Certification Tracks	Entry	Associate	Professional	Expert	Architect
Collaboration				CCIE Collaboration	
Data Center		CCNA Data Center	CCNP Data Center	CCIE Data Center	
Design	CCENT	CCDA	CCDP	CCDE	CCAr
Routing & Switching	CCENT	CCNA Routing and Switching	CCNP	CCIE Routing & Switching	
Security	CCENT	CCNA Security	CCNP Security	CCIE Security	
Service Provider		CCNA Service Provider	CCNP Service Provider	CCIE Service Provider	
Service Provider Operations	CCENT	CCNA Service Provider Operations	CCNP Service Provider Operations	CCIE Service Provider Operations	
Video		CCNA Video			
Voice	CCENT	CCNA Voice	CCNP Voice	CCIE Voice	
Wireless	CCENT	CCNA Wireless	CCNP Wireless	CCIE Wireless	

Figure 2- Cisco Certifications Track

About the CCNP Exam

- ➢ **Exam Number:** 300-206 CCNP
- ➢ **Associated Certifications:** CCNP Security
- ➢ **Duration:** 90 minutes (65-75 questions)
- ➢ **Exam Registration:** Pearson VUE

The Cisco Certified Network Professional (CCNP) Security Composite Exam (300-206) is a 90-minute, 65–75 question assessment that is associated with the CCNP Security certification. This exam tests a candidate's knowledge and skills related to technologies used to strengthen the security of a network perimeter such as Network Address Translation (NAT), ASA policy and application inspect, and a zone-based firewall on Cisco routers.

The following topics are general guidelines for the content likely to be included on the exam:

- ➢ Threat Defense: 25%
- ➢ Cisco Security Devices GUIs and Secured CLI Management: 25%
- ➢ Management Services on Cisco Devices: 12%
- ➢ Troubleshooting, Monitoring and Reporting Tools: 10%
- ➢ Threat Defense Architectures: 16%
- ➢ Security Components and Considerations: 12%

A complete list of topics covered in the CCNP exam.

How to Become CCNP Security?

Step 1: Pre-requisites

A valid CCNA Security certification or any CCIE certification can act as a pre-requisite.

Step 2: Prepare for the CCNA Exam

Exam preparation can be accomplished through self-study with textbooks, practice exams & on-site classroom programs. This workbook provides you all the information and knowledge to help pass the CCNP Security exam. Your study will be divided into two distinct parts:

1. Understanding the technologies as per exam blueprint.
2. Implementing and practicing the technologies on Cisco hardware.

IPSpecialist provides full support to enable the candidates for the challenging exam.

Step 3: Register for the Exam

Certification exams are offered at locations throughout the world. To register for an exam, contact Pearson VUE, the authorized test delivery partner of Cisco, who will administer the exam in a secured, proctored environment.

Decide which exam to take and note down the exam name and number. Refer to the Current Exam List webpage for exam details.

1. Gather personal information before exam registration:
   a. Legal Name (from government issued ID)
   b. Cisco Certification ID (i.e., CSCO000000001) or Test ID number
   c. Company Name
   d. Valid E-mail Address
   e. Method of Payment

2. If you have ever taken a Cisco exam before, please locate your Cisco Certification ID (i.e., CSCO000000001) before continuing with your registration to avoid duplicate records and delays in receiving proper credit for your exams.
3. A valid E-mail is required during exam registration. Cisco requires a valid E-mail to send E-mail reminders when a candidate's certification is about to expire, confirm the mailing address before shipping out the certificate and to inform candidates if their certificate was returned due to an incorrect address.
4. Pearson VUE is the Cisco authorized test delivery partner. You can register online, by telephone, or by walk-in (where available).

Q: How much does an exam cost?

Computer-based certification exam or written exam, prices depend on scope and exam length. Please refer to the "Exam Pricing" webpage for details.

Step4: Getting the Results

After you complete an exam at an authorized testing center, you will get an immediate online notification in the form of printed examination score report that indicates your pass or fail status, and your exam results section wise.

Congratulations!!! You are a CCNP Security Certified.

Chapter 01: Threat Defense

Technology Brief

Security is a broad topic, which should be discussed in everything we design, related to computer networking that may be wired or wireless. Network security has been considered important for quite some time, especially for those of us whose entire careers have been around the field of network security. There has been a surge in public awareness about securing their devices connected to the public internet because of events of data stealth and leakage in a past few years.

As new vulnerabilities and new methods of attack are being evolved, a least technical user can potentially launch a devastating attack against an unprotected network. As we strive to empower employees around the world with ubiquitous access to important data, it is increasingly important to take measures for the protection of data and the entities using it.

This section will start with mitigation techniques for common layer 2 attacks followed by the lab section, which explains the best practices for network device hardening.

Port Security

Port security is a very nice layer 2 feature of Cisco IOS, which allows network administrators to bind a specific number of MAC addresses to a specific port of networking device along with the violation action if a number of MAC address increases or a device, whose MAC address is not bound tries to connect to a port.

Just like router stores remote network entries in a routing table, a switch has its table known as Content Addressable Memory (CAM) table, which is a fancy word for MAC address table. When a switch is powered on, its CAM table has no entry in it. Whenever the first frame for specific destination hits the switch, it is then broadcasted to all active ports of that specific VLAN. If the destination MAC is alive and replies back, then its MAC along with the information of originating machine will be stored in the CAM table.

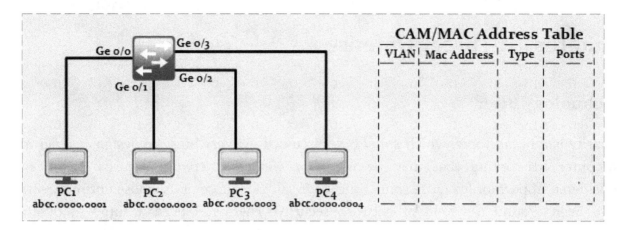

Figure 3- Switch with Empty CAM Table

Consider a situation where PC1 tries to send frames to PC3 as shown in Figure 4. In the first step, the switch will store the source MAC that is of PC1 in its CAM table. In the next step, it will check CAM table for destination MAC address. In case there is no entry present, the intended frame will be sent to all active ports (except the source port) to that specific VLAN. If PC3 replies back, then CAM table will be updated in the third step. Now any new frame, which is intended for PC3 will be unicast as the switch has its MAC in its CAM table.

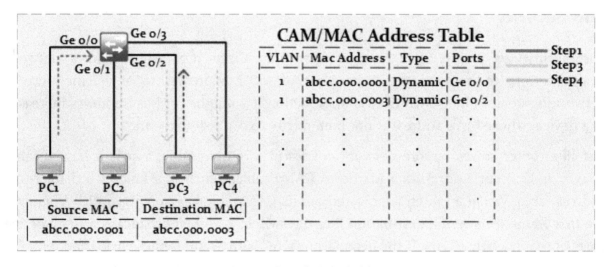

Figure 4- Switch with CAM Table Entries

CAM Table Overflow Attack

As everything is stored in Random Access Memory (RAM), every process has some processing and storage limitations. Just like routing table, CAM table has its own storage limitation (depending on hardware series). Let us say a switch can store only 50,000 entries in its CAM/Mac table at a time, if an attacker, say PC2, starts generating fraudulent MAC addresses using some tools present in *Kali Linux* then in a matter of time, the MAC counter will hit the maximum number. At this point, the switch will start acting as a HUB, which broadcasts anything hitting its interfaces. As a result, PC2 can run *Wireshark* and start analyzing the sessions between machines within LAN. This type of attack is referred to as CAM table overflow attack, and *port security* can be used to mitigate such kind of attacks.

Port Security Violation Actions

After detecting a fraudulent MAC address or a maximum number of MAC address allowed on the secured port, a port security feature can perform one of the actions as in Table 1.

Violation Action	Description
Protect	Discards the fraudulent or extra MAC address without notifying the administrator
Restrict	Discards the fraudulent or extra MAC address and generates Syslog message or SNMP trap. Alert generation feature of this action makes it preferable to the aforementioned action
Shutdown	Puts the port in err-disable state and everything gets discarded. Syslog/SNMP based alert is also generated in this case. However, it should be noted that shutdown is default violation action defined in Cisco IOS
Shutdown VLAN	Puts the VLAN in err-disable port for a port where the violation occurs. Syslog/SNMP based alert is also generated in this case.

Table 1- Port Security Violation Actions and their Descriptions

Port Security MAC Binding Techniques

In order to bind MAC address to specific switch port (which must be either in access or static trunk mode), the three options listed in Table 2 are available in Cisco IOS.

MAC Binding Options	Description
Dynamic	Port security feature dynamically learns the maximum allowable MAC addresses on switch-port on first come first serve basis. By default, only 1 MAC address is allowable on switch-port
Static	Manually binds the MAC address on switch-port. Preferred in a scenario where a number of secure ports are few
Sticky	This feature comes handy if a large number of secure ports require MAC binding. By using the sticky feature, the currently learned MAC addresses will be bound to the switch-ports and will get stored in running-configuration. A network administrator needs to save the running-configuration to startup-configuration so that these MACs get permanent as switch gets a reboot

Table 2- MAC Binding Options and their Descriptions

Port Security Drawbacks

Although a nice feature, but modern hacking tools can be used to spoof the MAC address and bypass this security check. Similarly, port security does not work with dynamically configured access or trunk ports. Switch port needs to be in static access or static trunk mode for port security to work. Modern security techniques such as the implementation of 802.1x are better and more secure ways of mitigating attacks related to layer 2 MAC addresses.

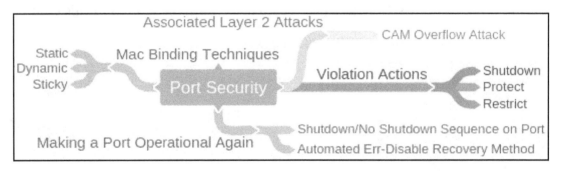

Figure 5- Port Security Mind Map

Storm Control

Storm control feature is used to mitigate situations where a huge number of packets flood through the network (either legitimate or fraudulent traffic). Apart from broadcast traffic, storm control feature can be used to limit multicast and even unicast traffic on Layer 2 port. In Table 3, few reasons behind the situation when switch or router experiences high network traffic are listed:

Reason	Description
Attacks (for example DOS/DDOS)	There may be some attack carried on a specific segment of a network, which may consume the processing power of networking device
Protocol Implementation	Some protocols may generate a tremendous amount of broadcast or multicast traffic, which may result in the unavailability of the network
Network Configuration Mismatch	Another very likely reason for traffic storm is accidental misconfiguration from network engineering. For example, disabling spanning tree may result in some endless loop within switching segment, etc.

Table 3- Reasons behind Traffic Storm and their Descriptions

Depending on the IOS version, storm control can be configured based on bandwidth percentage, packets per second (PPS) or bits per second (bps). Just like port security, storm control feature also performs one of the following action in case of violation.

Action	Description
Syslog Message	Configured as the default option, the device will drop the traffic exceeding the level defined by storm control feature and will generate Syslog message for it
SNMP Trap	Apart from above action, an additional SNMP trap will be generated
Shutdown	Storm control feature will put the port in the err-disable state on violation along with Syslog message generation. In order to make port functional again, shutdown/no shutdown sequence or auto recovery feature must be used

Table 4-Storm Control Response against Violation

DHCP Snooping

It is actually very easy for someone to bring accidentally or maliciously a DHCP server in a corporate environment. *DHCP Snooping* is all about protecting against it. Consider an instance of corporate network as in Figure 6- Rogue DHCP server in corporate environment:

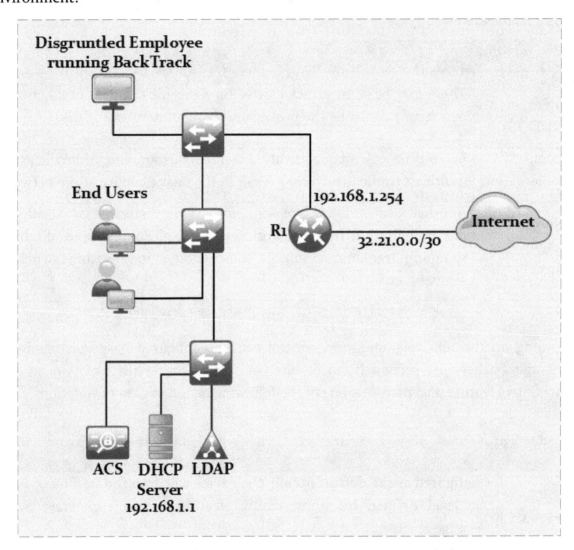

Figure 6- Rogue DHCP Server in a Corporate Environment

Shown in Figure 6, a DHCP server is running with an IP address of *192.168.1.1*. Let us consider a disgruntled employee say Bob who has some administrative issues in the office and has decided to bring an embedded device the following day to the office. On the embedded device, Bob has installed *BackTrack*, which is a *Linux* distribution commonly used for penetration testing and ethical hacking. Subsequently, Bob plugged the *BackTrack* based embedded device into his workstation's port and started listening to the

DHCP requests from different end-devices. A DHCP is a four-step (DORA) process as shown below:

D – Discover: Sent by end-devices for discovering DHCP server.

O – Offer: Response from DHCP server for corresponding *Discover* message.

R – Request: Sent by end-devices as a request for IP address to DHCP server.

A – Acknowledge: Response of DHCP server for the *Request* message.

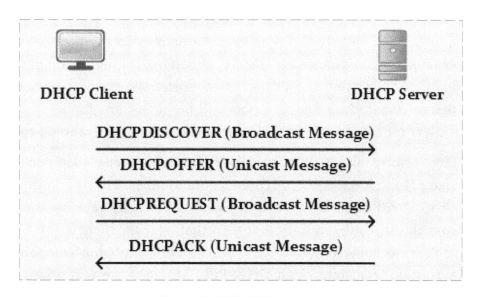

Figure 7- DHCP-DORA Process

Similarly, the client can send DHCPRELEASE packet to the server to make the assigned configuration available to some other client. Due to the broadcast nature of these steps, the request would be heard by both DHCP servers. Now, an IP address assigned by rouge DHCP server will also advertise itself to be the default gateway and DNS server as well. End-users who get an IP address from rogue DHCP server will never know about it as this process is done automatically and most of the employees do not have a deep understanding of how different networking services work. Now the disgruntled employee, after receiving the traffic, will send it to the correct gateway and successfully implement the *Man-in-the-Middle* attack.

DHCP Starvation Attack

Another possibility is launching the DHCP starvation attack. Considering the above scenario, the official corporate DHCP server can assign only 252 IP addresses (excluding DHCP itself and the default gateway address). Now there are tools available in *BackTrack Linux*, which can be used to send requests to DHCP server for IP address periodically.

Ultimately, after 252 assignments, DHCP server will run out of IP addresses, and corporate employees will end up having an IP address assigned from APIPA (169.254.0.0 address space) service.

In order to mitigate such attacks, DHCP snooping feature is enabled on networking devices to identify the only trusted ports from which DHCP traffic either in ingress or egress direction is considered legitimate. Any access port who tries to reply to the DHCP requests will be ignored because the device will only allow DHCP to process from the trusted port as defined by networking team.

When DHCP snooping is enabled with global configuration command, every port will be considered as un-trusted and trusted port must be defined in the next step with which legitimate DHCP server is connected. DHCP snooping feature can limit the DHCP messages from trusted as well as the untrusted ports. When the number of packets exceeds the defined limit, the respective port will be put in err-disable state. However, err-disable recovery procedure can be applied to make the port operational again.

DHCP snooping feature also maintains DHCP snooping table that contains client's information like MAC address, VLAN ID, and port number, etc. When device receives messages such as DHCPRELEASE message, which is normally sent by client to DHCP server to release the IP configuration bound to that specific client so that assigned IP address is available to some other DHCP client. DHCP snooping compares the MAC address and port numbers from which DHCPRELEASE message is received with DHCP snooping table to mitigate any kind of spoofing attempt. DHCP relay feature is used when the server is not present in LAN, i.e., DHCP server is running on some other network as shown in Figure 8:

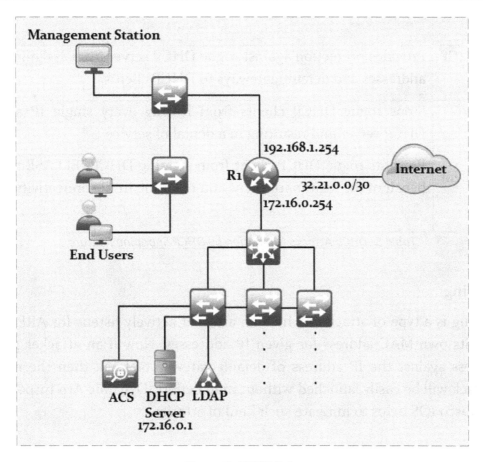

Figure 8- DHCP Relay

The GIADDR field in DHCP messages contains the IP address of relaying gateway. DHCP server uses the IP within GIADDR field to decide which DHCP scope should be used to assign an IP address to the requesting client. In case GIADDR field is set to some non-default value then this message will only be accepted on trusted ports. If switching segments are distributed as shown in Figure 8, where there is a hierarchy of distribution and access layers, then ports connected to distributed switch must also be set to trusted port.

Another option would be to use the global configuration command to accept the DHCP messages with zeros address in GIADDR field. Table 5 summarizes the mitigation techniques against DHCP attacks by DHCP snooping feature:

Attacks	Description
Rogue DHCP Server	Provides protection against rogue DHCP server from assigning illegal IP addresses and default gateways to DHCP clients
DHCP Starvation	Stops rogue DHCP clients from leasing every single IP available in DHCP server and resulting in a denial of service
DHCP Client Imposture	Prevents rogue DHCP client from sending DHCPRELEASE message on behalf of the legitimate client and resulting in IP connectivity issues

Table 5- DHCP Attacks Mitigation by DHCP Snooping Feature

ARP Spoofing

ARP spoofing is a type of attack in which an attacker actively listens for ARP broadcasts and sends its own MAC address for given IP addresses. Now if an attacker provides its MAC address against the IP address of default gateway of LAN, then the man-in-the-middle attack will be easily launched without much effort. Dynamic Arp Inspection (DAI) feature of Cisco IOS helps to mitigate such kind of attacks.

Man-in-the-Middle Attacks

Man-in-the-Middle (MITM) attacks happen when attackers break the normal link of communication between two nodes and act as a bridge between them. With the purpose of eavesdropping, it can happen both at TCP/IP Layer 2 and at Layer 3.

Attackers can use the concept of Address Resolution Protocol (ARP) poisoning so that devices on LAN consider attacker's MAC address to be the MAC address of the default gateway or some other machine inside LAN. The attacker will send the traffic to its correct destination, so that sender and receiver do not feel anything unusual happening between their sessions.

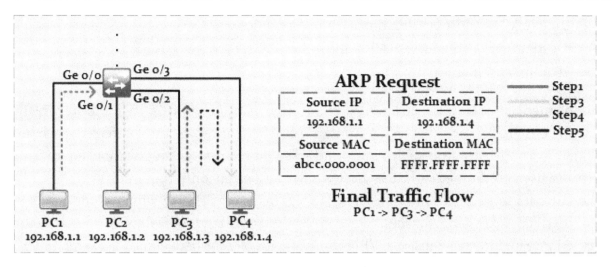

Figure 9- ARP Spoofing

In order to mitigate this attack, we need to enable Dynamic ARP Inspection (DAI) on switches. When DAI is enabled (as per VLAN), every port will be considered as an untrusted port. Global configuration command can be used to make specific ports as trusted ports from where ARP requests will not be inspected. When an ARP packet hits the switch from untrusted ports, it is compared against the DHCP snooping database for IP-to-MAC bindings. If no entry is present, then the ARP packet gets dropped. If DHCP is not running on LAN segment or DHCP snooping feature is not enabled, then ARP access-lists must be configured to allow ARP traffic. in order to do that, following steps must be performed:

- Just like IP based access-lists, create ARP based access lists using global configuration command of **arp access-list <access-list name>**
- Configure the permit/deny entries by **permit/deny IP host <sender-IP-address> mac host <sender-MAC-address> log** command
- As ARP inspection is performed per VLAN, the command to apply it per VLAN is **IP arp inspection filter <access-list-name> vlan <VLAN-ID> [static]**

DAI first checks whether ARP packet is legitimate or not by consulting ARP filter table, if there is no implicit deny statement in ARP access-list as well as no specific entry, then DHCP snooping table is checked for proper action to be applied on ARP packet.

Just liked DHCP snooping feature, DAI feature can limit ARP traffic on untrusted port with interface level command **IP arp inspection limit rate <pps> [burst interval <seconds>]**. On violation, port enters the err-disable state, which can be reverted by shutdown/no shutdown sequence or by applying err-disable automatic recovery feature.

Apart from above-mentioned features, DAI can perform additional checks that are:

- Source MAC address validation
- Destination MAC address validation
- IP address validation

To implement MITM attack at Layer 3, an attacker can introduce a rogue router in the network and make sure that other routers see this router as the preferred path for destination routes. To stop such kind of attacks, we can use authentication for routing protocols used in the network, use Access Lists to permit only required traffic, etc. To make our data more secure, we must use HTTPS instead of HTTP, which sends traffic in plain text. For accessing devices, we can use SSH instead of TELNET for a secure connection. Similarly, we must use VPNs for traffic to be sent between end-to-end nodes.

IP Source Guard

IP source guard feature is used to mitigate the IP spoofing and other related attacks. When enabled in layer 2 port, only traffic with a source IP address being defined in DHCP snooping table will be allowed. If DHCP or DHCP snooping is not enabled, then the static entry must be configured with global command **IP source binding <MAC-Address> VLAN <VLAN-ID> <IP-Address> interface <Interface-ID>.**

IP source guard feature can be configured to check either source IP address or a combination of source IP/MAC addresses.

MACSec

Media Access Control Security (MACSec) is an industry standard (IEEE 802.1AE), which provides confidentiality and integrity in conjunction with IEEE 802.1x standard. Implementing IEEE 802.1x along with MACSec provides identity-based access control at access layer of the network. Almost in every organization, consultants and guests require access to network resources over the same network as regular employees. There is also a possibility that guests may bring along unmanaged devices, which may result in access of unauthorized digital assets of the organization. Similarly, as the size of organization increases, the rate of such events increases exponentially.

IEEE 802.1x along with IEEE 802.1AE standard address such problems by implementing a three component base solution namely:

- **Supplicant:** It is the end-point device who wishes to connect LAN securely
- **Authenticator:** It is a network device (Cisco catalyst switch or some other supported device). It facilitates the whole process by relying on the credentials from end-point to

the server and then taking the corresponding action by either shutting down the port or opening it

- **Authentication Server:** It plays a key role in implementing IEEE 802.1x based port security and MACSec solution. It is typically a server running software that supports both RADIUS and EAP protocols. A common implementation of these protocols are NAP (Network Access Protection) role in *Microsoft Server* 2008 and 2012; Cisco ACS server also supports it and open source implementations like *FreeRadius* in Linux

Following are the benefits provided by MACSec in wired Ethernet environment:

Feature	Description
Confidentiality	Hop by Hop Layer 2 encryption provides confidentiality features
Integrity	Integrity feature makes sure that data is not changed on its way between communicating peers
Flexibility	By using centralized policy, MACSec can be enforced only on specific LAN segments while allowing the non-MACSec capable machines to access limited services

Table 6- MACSec Features

Just like any other feature, MACSec has some limitations as defined in Table 7:

Feature	Description
End-Points Support	Just like IEEE 802.1x, not every end-machine supports MACSec feature
Networking Hardware Support	Upgradation of access switches may be required as this feature is not supported on old switches
Technology Integration	Some services like IP telephony may be affected by integrating MACSec. Keeping every service in mind may be required for successful deployment

Table 7- MACSec Limitations

Figure 10 describes a high-level flow of IEEE 802.1x and MACSec:

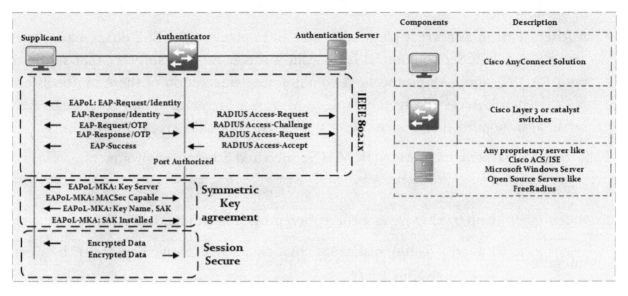

Figure 10- IEEE 802.1x and MACSec Sequence

Common Layer 2 Attacks and Best Practices for Mitigation

In order to implement the security techniques related to any switching concept, it is important to have a clear understanding of that technology otherwise many security flaws will remain there, which would create a problem in days to come. Following are the best security practices for overall network infrastructure, including layer 2 technologies:

- It is a good idea to change the native VLAN ID from the default value of 1 to some unused VLAN number
- Use of secure protocol, i.e., SSH instead of TELNET for remote management
- Port security feature should be used by allowing a limited number of MAC addresses on a single port
- DTP negotiation should be disabled to stop an attacker from making a trunk port with a switch
- Cisco Discovery Protocol (CDP) should be disabled to prevent an attacker getting the overall view of networking topology. CDP works at layer 2 and may help an attacker to redesign the attack according to the physical topology of the network. Similarly, if Link Layer Discovery (LLD) protocol is used, which is IEEE implementation of CDP, then it must be disabled as well
- When deploying new switch, shut down all unused ports and change the access VLAN assigned to them to some unused VLAN in the whole network
- Use of Control Plane Policing/Control Plane Protection
- Use of banners for a warning to be displayed on incoming connections

- Correct date and time stamp on log and debug messages
- Use of secure-boot set feature for start-up configuration and IOS of the device. If someone deletes the configuration or IOS, then this feature will allow using the backup files for restoration
- Authentication for routing protocols in use
- Disabling unused services in networking devices

This section explains different security measures along with their practical implementation in the lab section.

Use of Private VLANs

Using Private VLAN (PVLAN) provides the security and isolation features in some scenarios. Just like Ethernet VLANs, whose function is to break the broadcast domain into multiple smaller broadcast domains, PVLAN is used to further divide a single VLAN into sub-VLANs. PVLANs also require a layer three device like a router in order to communicate with some other VLAN. However, there are some differences as well. Unlike normal VLANs, which use a unique subnet for every broadcast domain, hosts in different PVLANs can belong to the same IP subnet while still requiring layer three devices for inter-PVLAN communication.

As an example, consider a normal Ethernet VLAN of 100, which is sub-divided in two private VLANs 101 and 102.

VLAN 100, which is a regular VLAN, is known as Primary VLAN. Ports assigned to normal and sub-divided VLAN will have one of the following types:

Promiscuous Mode: Normally connected to a router, this port is allowed to send and receive frames from any other port on the same VLAN.

Isolated Mode: As the name suggests, devices connected to isolated ports will only communicate with ports with Promiscuous Mode.

Community Mode: Community mode is used for a group of users who want communication between them. Community ports communicate with themselves and only with the Promiscuous mode.

In short, on the top of the hierarchy is the Primary VLAN that is the regular VLAN, 100 in the current scenario. It will be used to forward traffic from Promiscuous mode based ports to Isolated and Community mode based ports.

After Primary VLAN comes the secondary VLAN, which will be either Isolated or Community based on requirements.

Isolated VLAN: It forwards traffic from Isolated ports to Promiscuous ports.

Community VLAN: It forwards traffic within community ports and to the promiscuous ports.

PVLANs are normally used in shared environments like ISP colocation where the same subnet may be used for all customers, but their traffic is logically isolated from each other due to PVLANs.

BPDU Guard

Understanding this feature without any knowledge of how the spanning tree works and what does BPDU mean, would a bit challenging. Spanning tree protocol (STP) is a layer 2 technology, and its function is to make a loop-free network at Layer 2 of TCP/IP stack. STP does this by selecting a *Root Bridge* in a network and making a loop-free network with respect to *Root Bridge*. Like every other protocol, selecting root bridge is done by comparing some parameters of every single layer 2 device in a network. This parameter is known as Bridge Protocol Data Unit (BPDU). Inside BPDU is the MAC address of a device and 2-byte value known as Bridge Priority.

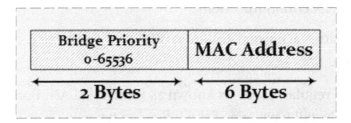

Figure 11- BPDU Packet Arrangement

By default, Bridge Priority is 32768, which can be changed later. Every switch shares BPDU with other switches. Switch with lower Bridge ID will become the root bridge. As Default Bridge Priority is same on all devices, so the MAC address becomes the focal point of STP elections in default conditions. A switch with lowest MAC address will become the root bridge.

Consider the following switch segment as STP, election for root bridge is about to happen.

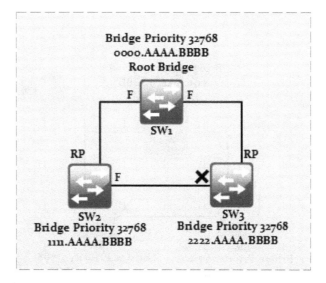

Figure 12- STP Root Bridge Election Process

Switch *SW1* is elected as Root Bridge due to its lowest MAC address hence best bridge ID. Now, every traffic forwarding will be done via *SW1*. In the next step, root port will be selected on remaining switches, which is selected according to the best path cost to the root bridge. In the third step, remaining ports are checked, and specific ports will be shut down to make the network a loop-free.

In the above discussion, the importance of BPDU packet is obvious. If an attacker gets a chance to connect a switch to above switch segment and sends illegal BPDU packets stating itself to have best BPDU guard, all switches will align themselves according to it.

In order to prevent this situation, BPDU guard feature must be enabled on access ports, which disables the port in case of any BPDU packet seen in the inbound direction. Once a port is disabled due to BPDU violation, it will show err-disabled state. To bring the interface back up again, *shutdown* command must be issued followed by *no shutdown* command.

Root Guard

Apart from BPDU Guard, if there is administrative limitation within an organization and switch from someone's administrative domain is connected to another switch whose configuration and management is someone else's responsibility, then *Root Guard* is enabled on ports connecting to another switch to prevent the STP topology by ignoring messages related to new root switch on that port

Loop Guard

Loop Guard feature helps to prevent loop creation after STP is converged and redundant links are disabled.

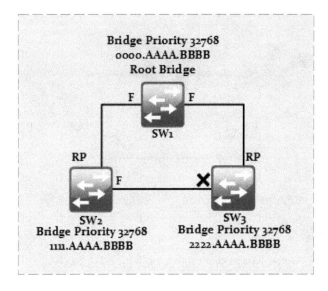

Figure 13- Loop Creation after STP Convergence

Consider the above diagram, let us say that port of switch *SW2* gets down due to any reason then the err-disabled port of switch SW3 may come up and enter into the forwarding state. If this port of switch SW2 comes up again, then the loop is again created in the above switching segment. STP will take some time to converge again. In order to prevent such situations, *Loop Guard* feature must be enabled on a port, which disables the port in case no BPDU packet is received on it.

Common Layer 2 Attacks Mind Map

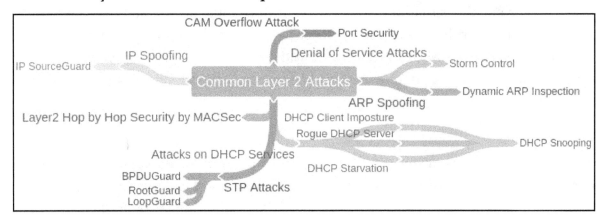

Figure 14- Common Layer 2 Attack's Mind Map

Network Address Translation (NAT)

NAT is one the most widely used feature in Cisco devices. Figure 15 acts as a reference for discussion in this section.

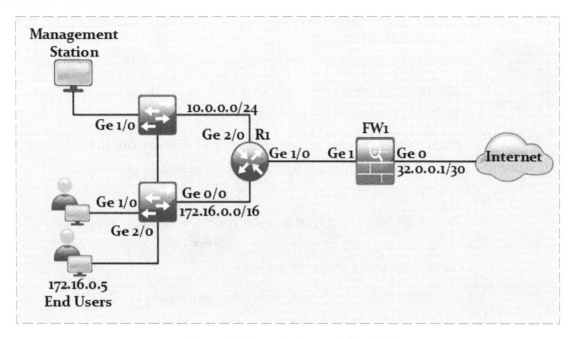

Figure 15- Example Scenario for NAT

As shown in above diagram, end-users along with management network is using the private addressing scheme as defined in RFC 1918. If an end-user wants to talk with any end-devices out there on the internet, a public IP address would be needed. The firewall does not have any connectivity problem because of globally reachable IP address of 32.0.0.1/30 assigned to one of its interfaces. In order to allow the internal or trusted network to communicate with the public internet, NAT feature is used by either firewall or router by swapping the source address field in IP header of originating packets with either its own global address or with a pool of global addresses (assigned by service providers).

The implementation of NAT or Port Address Translation (PAT) not only hides thousands of users behind single or group of global IP addresses but also helps in mitigating some types of attack. Without knowing that which global IP address is assigned to the internal device, connecting with the specific internal device from the outside world is even more difficult.

NAT Terminologies: In Cisco's implementation of NAT, either in routers or firewalls, very specific terminologies are used, for example inside local, outside global, etc. Table 8 summarizes the different terminologies of NAT/PAT.

NAT Term	Description
Inside Local	The original IP address of the host from the trusted network. For example, 172.16.0.5 has been assigned to end users in the above diagram
Inside Global	The global address either a router's interface IP or one from the pool, which will represent the client out on the internet
Outside Local	The IP address with which a device is known on the internet. For example, the IP cameras, which are configured to be accessed anywhere from the internet
Outside Global	The real IP address of host device that is configured to be accessed over the internet. Like the private IP address of IP camera, which will be accessed via some global IP address

Table 8- NAT Terminologies and their Descriptions

Port Address Translation (PAT): It is a *subset* of NAT. Instead of representing each unique private IP address with unique global or real IP address, PAT uses a combination of different port numbers with unique IP addresses. Port numbers may vary from 1024 to 65535 which look enough for one's need. However, in case the number of sessions exceeds than the total port numbers, PAT will use the next globally available IP address from the pool, if available.

Table 9 summarizes the different NAT/PAT types and their description.

Options	Description
Static NAT	Static NAT maps one internal IP to one globally reachable IP address. For example, if the internal LAN consists of 100 users, then 100 global IP addresses will be needed for each of them to be able to communicate over the internet. Since this is not the feasible option for LAN users; this option is normally used for special cases such as for servers available in Demilitarized Zone (DMZ), which are accessed publically by general users. By using the static one-to-one mapping of server's original IP address with one of the global IP addresses from POOL and then entering the global IP address in DNS table, users can access it by name for example www.ipspecialist.net

Dynamic NAT	Dynamic NAT is used where users may need to send traffic at small intervals. As a result, the router can dynamically assign that address to some other user or end-device who needs the global address for sending traffic to the public internet. However, traffic may be dropped for extra clients when every global IP address from the pool is assigned to internal devices. In order to avoid such situations, dynamic PAT is used. For example, a pool of six global IP address can serve only six internal LAN users at a time. Client coming in the seventh number will have to wait for one of the global address to be released and assigned to it
Dynamic PAT	This option is widely used for internal LAN users who want to have internet access. By using the single IP assigned to the router interface along with the range of Port numbers that vary from 1024 to 65535, thousands of users can hide behind it. In normal scenarios, single IP address is enough to serve the broad range of users, however another IP address from a global address pool, if available, can be used in case of shortage of ports along with one IP address
Policy NAT/PAT	In this type, NAT/PAT is performed only when specific traffic is generated, matched by Access-List. Traffic without any match will be forwarded without NAT/PAT

Table 9- NAT/PAT Types and their Description

Consider the scenario where a client with IP address 172.16.0.5 wants some web surfing. As private IP addresses (defined in RFC 1918) are not routable in internet cloud, one option is to implement NATing on first hop device (Router) or edge device of an organization (firewall in our case). The NAT table, which will be created on the respective device will look like Table 10:

Original Source IP	Translated Source IP	Source Port	Destination IP	Destination Port
172.16.0.5	32.21.0.1	41101	8.8.8.8	80
172.16.0.5	32.21.0.1	41102	8.8.8.8	80
172.16.0.5	32.21.0.1	41103	8.8.8.8	80

Table 10- NAT Conversion

One of the *advantages* of using NAT is hiding the internal IP scheme of an organization, which along with other security practices may help in mitigating the overall attack

scenario because the attacker will need to find the conversion of private to public IP and associated port before launching the attack.

Traffic Filtering by using Access-Lists

As the name depicts, Access Control Lists (ACLs) are used primarily for traffic filtering coming either egress or ingress from an interface. Access-lists are also used in a number of instances for example route filtering, policy-based routing, Quality of Service (QoS), etc. Inside an ACL, are internally organized Access-Control Entries (ACEs), which perform the action of permitting the traffic or discarding it. Whenever traffic hits the interface, the respective ACL configured on that interface starts checking for an intended match from top to bottom fashion. If no entry is found, the traffic is denied as there is implicit deny at the end of every access-list.

The following table shows the major categories of IP based ACL:

ACL Type	Description
Standard ACL	Standard ACLS ranges between 1-99 and only source IP address can be used in the ACEs. Standard ACLs are always preferred near to destination. Standard ACLs are normally used for limiting the management access of VTY lines in Cisco IOS
Extended ACL	Extended ACLs ranged between 100-199 and provided granular control for traffic by using Layer3 and Layer4 information. Extended ACLs are always preferred near to source
Named ACL	Named ACLs are either standard or extended in nature. The only difference that exists is the ease, by which Named ACLs can be reconfigured. Named ACL assigns an incremental number (increment of 10 by default) to the ACEs, which can be further used to delete a specific entry from ACL
Time-based ACL	Time-based ACL are also standard or extended in nature. The only difference that exists is the association of Time-Range with an ACL, which defines the time when this should be applied on whichever interface is configured for it
Reflexive ACL	Reflexive ACLs are a little bit dynamic in nature as they create temporary entries and filtering action is performed based on sessions information

Table 11- Types of ACL and their Descriptions

MAC Access-Lists

Just like IP based ACLs, MAC ACL is applied on layer 2 port of switches to filter (deny or permit) features like ARP, STP or any other layer 2 protocol based on its Ether-type value. Creating MAC-based ACL is almost same as of IP based ACL. From global configuration mode, the **mac access-list extended <ACL-Name>** command is used first to create an ACL. Following parameters are used to create Access-Control Entries (ACE) of MAC-based ACLs: **deny|permit <Source-MAC> <Destination-MAC> <Non-IP-Protocol>**. Unlike IP based ACLs, MAC ACL can only be applied in the inbound direction.

Switch-Port Access-Lists

When IP based ACL is applied to Layer 2 switch port in the inbound direction, it is called Port ACL (PACL). Unlike IP based ACL on Layer 3 device, PACL is applicable only in the inbound direction.

VLAN Access-Lists

Being applied on VLAN itself, VLAN ACL (VACL) can be used to filter both IP and non-IP based traffic. A VLAN is created at the software level, VACL does not require inbound or outbound direction in order to perform its action. In order to implement VACL, first, we need to create MAC based or IP based ACL for non-IP or IP based traffic respectively. In the second step we need to create VLAN access-map rule (similar to route-map) for IP and/or non-IP based traffic (by calling respective ACLs). In the third step, VLAN access-map is associated with the desired VLAN to perform its action.

Adaptive Security Appliance (ASA)

The primary function of using a dedicated device named as the *firewall* at the edge of the corporate network is isolation. A firewall prevents the direct connection of internal LAN with internet or outside world. This isolation can be performed in multiple ways but not limited to:

A Layer 3 device using an Access List for restricting the specific type of traffic on any of its interfaces.

A Layer 2 device using the concept of VLANs or Private VLANs (PVLAN) for separating the traffic of two or more networks.

A dedicated host device with software installed on it. This host device, also acting as a proxy, filters the desired traffic while allowing the remaining traffic.

Although above features provide isolation in some sense, following are the few reasons listed in Table 12, a dedicated firewall appliance (either in hardware or software) is preferred in production environments:

Risks	Protection by Firewall
Access by Untrusted Entities	Firewall tries to categorize the network into different portions. One portion is considered as a trusted portion of internal LAN. Public internet and interfaces connected to are considered as an untrusted portion. Similarly, servers accessed by untrusted entities are placed in a special segment known as a Demilitarized Zone (DMZ). By allowing only specific access of these servers, like port 90 of the web server, firewall hides the functionality of network device that makes it difficult for an attacker to understand the physical topology of the network
Deep Packet Inspection and Protocols Exploitation	One of the cool features of the dedicated firewall is its ability to inspect the traffic more than just IP and port level. By using digital certificates, Next Generation Firewalls available today can inspect traffic up to layer 7. A firewall can also limit the number of established as well as half-open TCP/UDP connections to mitigate DDoS attacks
Access Control	By implementing local AAA or by using ACS/ISE servers, the firewall can permit traffic based on AAA policy
Antivirus and Protection from Infected Data	By integrating IPS/IDP modules with firewall, malicious data can be detected and filtered at the edge of the network to protect the end-users

Table 12- Firewall Risk Mitigation Features

Although firewall provides great security features as discussed in Table 12, however, any misconfiguration or bad network design may result in serious consequences. Another important deciding factor of deploying a firewall in current network design depends on whether current business objectives can bear the following limitations:

Misconfiguration and its Consequences: The primary function of a firewall is to protect network infrastructure in a more elegant way than a traditional layer 3/2 devices. Depending on different vendors and their implementation techniques, many features need to be configured for a firewall to work properly. Some of these features may include Network Address Translation (NAT), Access-Lists (ACLs), AAA based policies and so on. Misconfiguration of any of these features may result in leakage of digital assets, which may have a financial impact on business. In short, complex devices like firewall also

requires deep insight knowledge of equipment along with the general approach to deployment.

Applications and Services Support: Most of the firewalls use different techniques to mitigate the advanced attacks. For example, NATing is one of the most commonly used features in firewalls, and it is used to mitigate the reconnaissance attacks. In situations where network infrastructure is used to support custom-made applications, it may be required to re-write the whole application in order to properly work under new network changes.

Latency: Just like implementing NATing on a route adds some end-to-end delay, firewall along with heavy process demanding features add a noticeable delay over the network. Although high-end devices of Cisco Adaptive Security Appliance (ASA) series and other vendor's equipment have a very small throughput delay, some applications like Voice over IP (VoIP) may require special configuration to deal with it.

Another important factor to be considered while designing the security policies of network infrastructure is to use the layered approach instead of relying on a single element. For example, consider the scenario as in Figure 16:

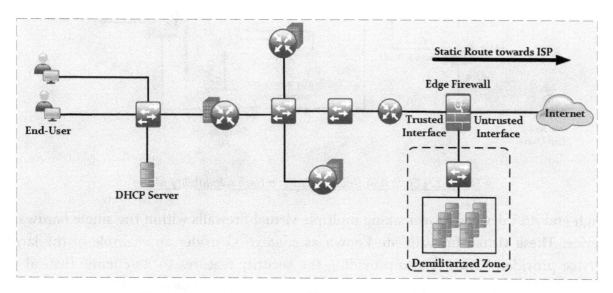

Figure 16- Positioning Firewall in a Production Environment

The position of firewall varies in different design variants. In some designs, it is placed after the perimeter router of the corporation while in some designs it is placed at the edge of the network as shown in Figure 15. Irrelevant to the position, it is a good practice to implement the layered security in which some of the features like unicast reverse path forwarding, access-lists, etc. are enabled on perimeter routers. Features like deep packet

inspection, digital signatures are matched on the firewall. If everything looks good, the packet is allowed to hit the intended destination address.

High Availability and Security Context: Just like First Hop Routing Protocols can be used on Cisco routers to provide load balancing and redundancy as well; two firewalls can be combined to provide similar results. In case one device goes down due to any software or hardware failure, the second device will take its place. Two of the most common configurations of implementing high availability are Active/Standby failover and Active/Active failover. In Active/Standby failover, one device will act as a primary firewall or active firewall while the second one will be in standby mode. Just like HSRP, the standard protocol traffic will be exchanged periodically between firewalls to check the status of active and standby firewalls. As shown in Figure 17, Ge 0/3 link will be used for the transmission of failover information. In case active firewall goes down, standby firewall will immediately take the charge.

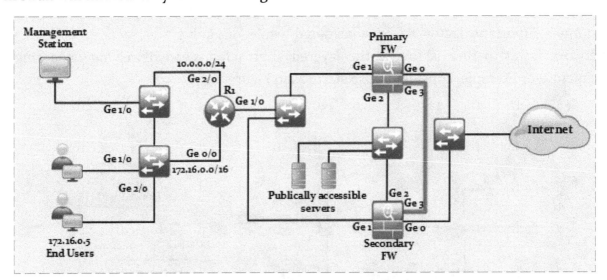

Figure 17- Cisco ASA Deployment in a High Availability Mode

High-end ASA devices allow making multiple virtual firewalls within the single hardware device. These virtual firewalls are known as *context*. Consider an example of the large service provider, which is also providing the security features to its clients. Instead of using single hardware firewall for each client connection, service providers can use one high-end firewall and create multiple contexts in it. In this way, each client will be assumed to have a separate piece of hardware as his/her next hop, and traffic will be isolated virtually from one hardware device. In active/active failover, physical connection may remain same as active/standby failover, so instead we make one firewall to act as primary for one context and second firewall to be primary for the second context just like HSRP can be tweaked to use multiple routers at the same time by making each router active for one unique VLAN.

Case Study

Multinational Mobile TV Streaming Company has its main office in Ireland and several branch offices spanning across the UK. Every branch office connects to the main office via *Site to Site* or *Remote VPN* over the public internet. Everything was working fine till one morning when the streaming service got terribly slow. With initial investigation, it came to the light that core router's CPU process is hitting above 95% and packet flow was not taking optimal path within switching segments. Further investigation also revealed fraudulent networking devices acting as focal point of switching segment. One of the project managers who has some prior knowledge about the cyber-attacks and leakage of sensitive information has ordered you to overview the current security posture of the main office and take necessary actions as required. Figure 18 shows the topology for one of the segments of the overall main office network.

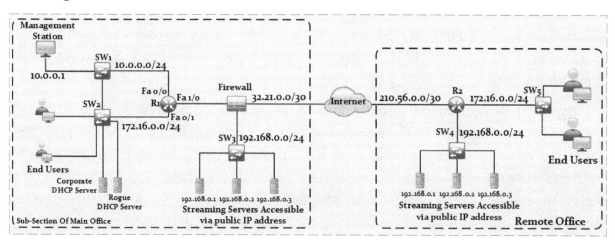

Figure 18- Threat Defense Case Study

Lab 1.1: Basic Passwords Setting and Filtering Remote Access

Cisco routers, switches and firewalls come with no password set on login interfaces. Some variants come with username set to *Cisco* and password set to *Cisco*. Whenever, a user tries to log in either via console port, Telnet/SSH session, it gets to *level 1* access where basic command set is available. One of the commonly used command at level 1 shows command used to show various important information like IP addresses assigned to each interface. When a user enters *enable* command at level 1, it gets the level 15 access where complete access of device is available. Now a user can enter into the global configuration of Cisco IOS by typing *configure terminal* and can change anything. Two important access usernames/passwords identified in above discussion are:

Level 1 username/password prompt: Level 1 access must be allowed after successful attempt of correct username and password. Because an attacker can get various information, which can result in reconnaissance attacks.

Enable/level 15 password: If an attacker accesses level 15 of the device, implementation of whole security posture is of no good use. Previous versions of Cisco IOS supports *enable password* command. This command is replaced with *enable secret* command, which increases the security of password phrase by storing it in hashed form in configuration. *Enable password* command stores password in plain text. Additional command of *service password-encryption* is used to store passwords in hashed form, but it can be cracked with simple methods.

Another important aspect of accessing the device remotely is using SSH instead of Telnet. *Wireshark* is a common sniffing tool used to follow the TCP/UDP streams. Telnet does not use encryption, which can result in *Man-in-the-Middle* attacks. To enable SSH on Cisco devices, *hostname* and *domain name* is mandatory to be configured before generating RSA keys for SSH. Hostname and domain name can be set in global configuration mode.

Management access should also be limited to specific IP addresses of management station. By entering *line VTY* command in global configuration mode, a user gets into special configuration mode related to remote access of Cisco device. A number of Telnet/SSH sessions a device can make depends on the specific model number and its series. By entering special configuration mode, the *access-class* command is used to call Access List in an inward direction to allow only management station to access device.

Let us implement the above concepts on the only router shown in Figure 18. The number of routers and switches may increase, but the basic concept of security remains the same.

Let us assume that management station has IP address of *10.0.0.1*. Last IP address from each subnet is assigned on router's interfaces. As Cisco devices come with a clean configuration, we need to access the device via console port for the first time to implement the concepts defined above.

Configuration:

R1:

Enter the level 15 by entering enable on user privilege mode

R1>enable

Enter configure terminal to enter the global configuration mode

R1#configure terminal

Use enable secret command to set the level 15 password

Use a long string of password with multiple character types

R1(config)# enable secret 0 P@$$word:10

Define a username and password with associated privilege level

R1(config)#username IPSpecialist privilege 1 secret 0 P@$$word:10

Set the hostname of your choice

R1(config)#hostname R1

Set the domain name for SSH to work

R1(config)#IP domain name IPSpecialist.net

R1(config)#crypto key generate rsa general-keys modulus 1024

Set the SSH version to 2

R1(config)#IP ssh version 2

Go to the line console sub configuration mode to set authentication

R1(config)#line console 0

R1(config-line)#login local

Similarly, go to the line vty sub configuration mode to do the same

R1(config)#line vty 0 903

R1(config-line)# login local

Enable the only SSH. Disable Telnet for being less secure

R1(config-line)# transport input ssh

R1(config-line)# Also call access list to limit access to only to management-station

R1(config-line)#access-class MGMT-STATION in

Now define MGMT-STATION named based ACL

R1(config)#IP access-list standard MGMT-STATION

R1(config-std-nacl)#permit host 10.0.0.1

```
Go to line aux sub configuration mode
```

R1(config)#line aux 0

R1(config-line)# login local

Verification

Open Putty on management pc. Enter router's IP address. Management PC should be able to access the router through SSH.

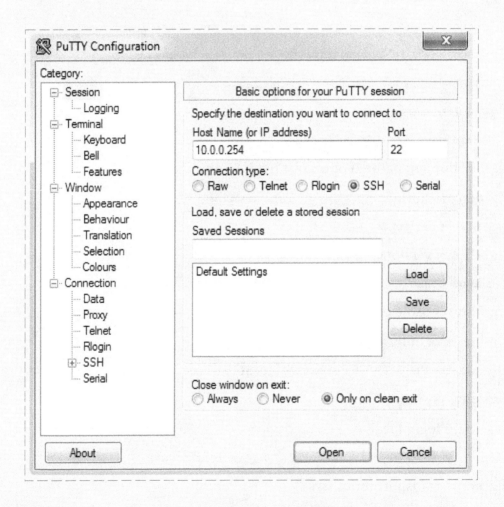

Click "Open" and user will be prompted for login username. Enter the above "IPSpecialist" as username and "P@$$word:10" as a password. The user will also be prompted with Putty security alert. Click "Yes" to continue.

After entering username and password, the user should get Level 1 access. Enter Level 15 by entering enable command and providing the above-defined password.

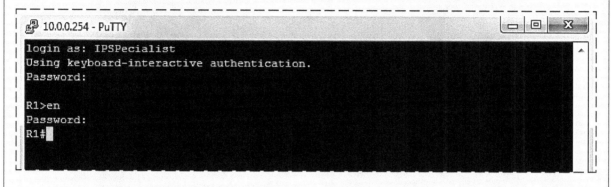

Now, close this connection and use telnet instead. The user should not be able to connect as SSH is the only allowed option.

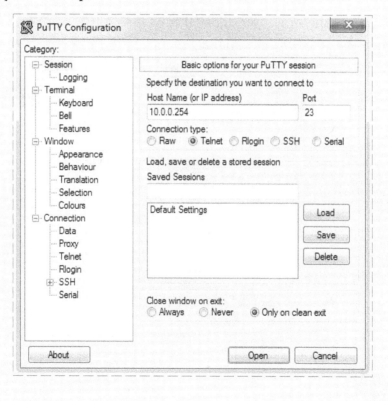

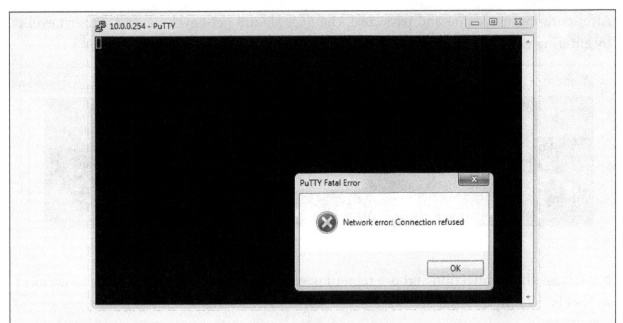

Management Station is the only user allowed to access router with 10.0.0.1 as the source IP address. Change the IP address of Management Station to verify it. Change IP address of *Local Area Connection 2* to 10.0.0.2 and SSH will not work this time.

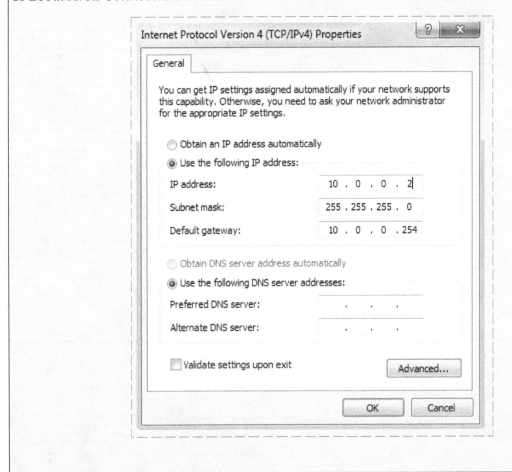

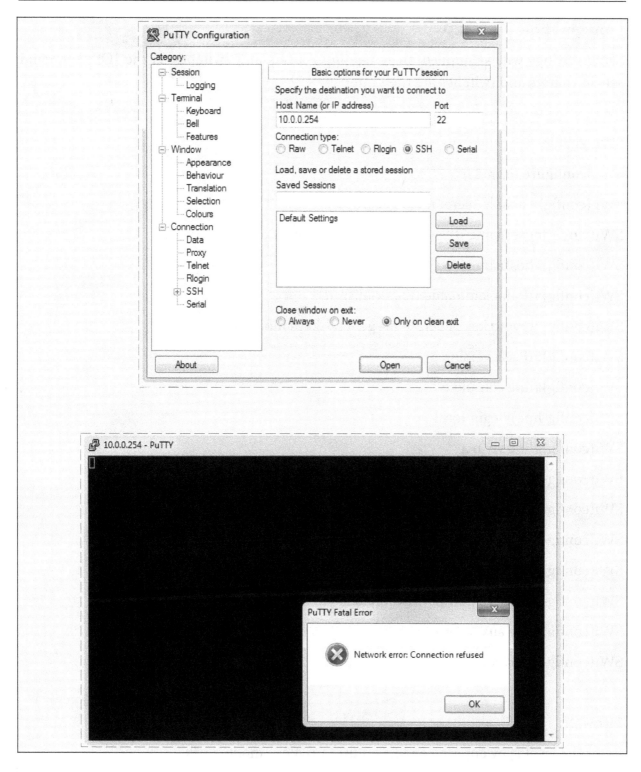

Configuration:

Same settings will be applied on remaining routers and switches as the IOS command sets in routers and switches are the same.

SW1:

SW1>enable

SW1#configure terminal

SW1 (config)# enable secret 0 P@$$word:10

SW1(config)#username IPSpecialist privilege 1 secret 0 P@$$word:10

SW1(config)#hostname SW1

SW1(config)#IP domain name IPSpecialist.net

SW1(config)#crypto key generate rsa general-keys modulus 1024

SW1(config)#IP ssh version 2

SW1(config)#line console 0

SW1(config-line)#login local

SW1(config)#line vty 0 4

SW1(config-line)# login local

SW1(config-line)# transport input ssh

SW1(config-line)#access-class MGMT-STATION in

SW1(config)#IP access-list standard MGMT-STATION

SW1(config-std-nacl)#permit host 10.0.0.1

SW1(config)#line aux 0

SW1(config-line)# login local

Firewall:

Enter the level 15 by entering enable on user privilege mode

FIREWALL>enable

Password:

Press Enter as no password is set up to this point.

```
Enter configure terminal to enter the global configuration mode
```

FIREWALL #configure terminal

FIREWALL(config)#int eth 0

FIREWALL(config-if)#nameif inside

FIREWALL(config-if)#no shutdown

```
Use enable password command to set the level 15 password
```

FIREWALL(config)# enable password P@$$word:10 level 15

```
Define a username and password with associated privilege level
```

FIREWALL(config)# username IPSpecialist password P@$$word:10 privilege 1

In order to restrict the remote connections to specific IP address, let us say only 10.0.0.1 can access FIREWALL from the interface with name "inside", use the following commands:

FIREWALL(config)# ssh 10.0.0.1 255.255.255.255 inside

```
Just like routing and switching devices, the crypto key needs to be generated for
SSH.
```

FIREWALL(config)# domain-name ipspecialist.net

FIREWALL(config)# crypto key generate rsa general-keys modulus 1024

```
In the last step, AAA authentication for SSH must be defined. As no TACACS/RADIUS
server is used in this lab, so LOCAL AAA settings will be used.
```

FIREWALL(config)# aaa authentication ssh console LOCAL

FIREWALL(config)#route inside 10.0.0.0 255.255.255.0 1.1.1.1

Verification

Open Putty on management PC. Enter Firewall's IP address, i.e., 1.1.1.2. Management PC should be able to access the firewall through SSH.

Show SSH session command can be used to verify the active SSH sessions with FIREWALL.

```
1.1.1.2 - PuTTY                                                        _ □ ×
FIREWALL#
FIREWALL#
FIREWALL# sho ssh sessions

SID Client IP        Version Mode Encryption Hmac    State          Username
0   10.0.0.1         2.0     IN   aes256-cbc sha1    SessionStarted IPSpecialist
                             OUT  aes256-cbc sha1    SessionStarted IPSpecialist
1   10.0.0.1         2.0     IN   aes256-cbc sha1    SessionStarted IPSpecialist
                             OUT  aes256-cbc sha1    SessionStarted IPSpecialist
FIREWALL#
```

In this lab, secure access and remote filtering have been done on main office's devices. Remote Office's devices will be configured in the last section of this lab.

Lab 1.2: Implementation of NAT/PAT Types on Cisco ASA

In this lab, topology from the last lab will be used.

Static NAT

Before implementing Static NAT for management and remote LAN of the main office, let us ping simulated internet (32.21.0.2) from management station (10.0.0.1). As internet router does not have routes for inside networks; it will not be able to route packets destined for 10.0.0.0/24 and 172.16.0.0/24 networks. *debug IP packets* command on ISP1 the router will show the following results:

ISP1#debug IP packet

```
IP packet debugging is on
ISP1#

*Mar   1 00:02:50.839:  IP:  tableid=0,  s=10.0.0.1 (FastEthernet0/0),  d=32.21.0.2
(FastEthernet0/0), routed via RIB

*Mar    1  00:02:50.839:   IP:   s=10.0.0.1   (FastEthernet0/0),   d=32.21.0.2
(FastEthernet0/0), len 60, rcvd 3

*Mar  1 00:02:50.839: IP: s=32.21.0.2 (local), d=10.0.0.1, len 60, unroutable
```

To work around this problem, Static NAT for management PC will be implemented.

FIREWALL(config)# object network MANAGEMENT-STATION

FIREWALL (config-network-object)# host 10.0.0.1

FIREWALL (config-network-object)# NAT (inside,outside) static 12.12.12.12

49

The first command creates a network object with the name MANAGEMENT-STATION. The second command defines a host with IP address 10.0.0.1, which is the IP address of the management station. The third command actually implements the static NAT for the management station. The "(inside, outside)" shows the direction of originating traffic, i.e., from inside interface to outside interface. The *static* 12.12.12.12 command tells the ASA to use 12.12.12.12 as source address for traffic that originates from management station towards network attached to outside zone or interface.

Ping 32.21.0.2 from management station again. This time ISP1 will send reply as 12.12.12.12. It will be used as source address from FIREWALL, which is also advertised in Simulated Internet.

```
*Mar   1 00:25:48.375: IP: tableid=0, s=12.12.12.12 (FastEthernet0/0), d=32.21.0.2
(FastEthernet0/0), routed via RIB

*Mar     1  00:25:48.375:   IP:   s=12.12.12.12   (FastEthernet0/0),   d=32.21.0.2
(FastEthernet0/0), len 60, rcvd 3

*Mar   1  00:25:48.379:  IP:  tableid=0,  s=32.21.0.2  (local),  d=12.12.12.12
(FastEthernet0/0), routed via FIB

*Mar   1 00:25:48.379: IP: s=32.21.0.2 (local), d=12.12.12.12 (FastEthernet0/0), len
60, sending

*Mar   1 00:25:49.423: IP: tableid=0, s=12.12.12.12 (FastEthernet0/0), d=32.21.0.2
(FastEthernet0/0), routed via RIB

*Mar     1  00:25:49.423:   IP:   s=12.12.12.12   (FastEthernet0/0),   d=32.21.0.2
(FastEthernet0/0), len 60, rcvd 3

*Mar   1  00:25:49.423:  IP:  tableid=0,  s=32.21.0.2  (local),  d=12.12.12.12
(FastEthernet0/0), routed via FIB

*Mar   1 00:25:49.423: IP: s=32.21.0.2 (local), d=12.12.12.12 (FastEthernet0/0), len
60, sending

*Mar   1 00:25:50.467: IP: tableid=0, s=12.12.12.12 (FastEthernet0/0), d=32.21.0.2
(FastEthernet0/0), routed via RIB

*Mar     1  00:25:50.467:   IP:   s=12.12.12.12   (FastEthernet0/0),   d=32.21.0.2
(FastEthernet0/0), len 60, rcvd 3

*Mar   1  00:25:50.467:  IP:  tableid=0,  s=32.21.0.2  (local),  d=12.12.12.12
(FastEthernet0/0), routed via FIB
```

Dynamic NAT

In order to perform Dynamic NAT, publically routable IP pool is required. Let us say that ! pool is 12.12.12.0/29. It means six IP addresses can be used from this pool. Let us use this ! pool for Main Office End-users LAN.

FIREWALL(config)# object network DYNAMIC-NAT-POOL

FIREWALL(config-network-object)# range 12.12.12.1 12.12.12.6

```
The above commands create a range of IP addresses, which will used as source IP for
End-User LAN PCs.
```

FIREWALL(config)# object network END-USER-NAT

FIREWALL(config-network-object)# subnet 172.16.0.0 255.255.255.0

FIREWALL(config-network-object)# NAT (inside, outside) dynamic DYNAMIC-NAT-POOL

```
Above commands create NAT rule for 172.16.0.0/24 subnet with dynamic NAT by using !
DYNAMIC-NAT-POOL defined above.
```

Verification

In order to verify Dynamic NAT, ping 32.21.0.2 from END-USER LAN, public IP pool is advertised in simulated internet LAN and it will be used in source IP address field, END-USER LAN should be able to get PING results as shown below:

VPCS> ping 32.21.0.2

```
84 bytes from 32.21.0.2 icmp_seq=1 ttl=254 time=72.131 ms

84 bytes from 32.21.0.2 icmp_seq=2 ttl=254 time=32.986 ms

84 bytes from 32.21.0.2 icmp_seq=3 ttl=254 time=23.358 ms

84 bytes from 32.21.0.2 icmp_seq=4 ttl=254 time=29.205 ms

84 bytes from 32.21.0.2 icmp_seq=5 ttl=254 time=32.147 ms
```

Similarly, show xlate command can be used at firewall to see currently established connections.

FIREWALL# show xlate

```
2 in use, 2 most used

Flags: D - DNS, e - extended, I - identity, i - dynamic, r - port map,
```

```
          s - static, T - twice, N - net-to-net
NAT from inside:10.0.0.1 to outside:12.12.12.12

    flags s idle 0:02:41 timeout 0:00:00

NAT from inside:172.16.0.1 to outside:12.12.12.6 flags i idle 0:02:02 timeout 3:00:00
```

Similarly show NAT command can be used to see NAT translations

FIREWALL# show NAT

```
Auto NAT Policies (Section 2)

1 (inside) to (outside) source static MANAGEMENT-STATION 12.12.12.12

    translate_hits = 7, untranslate_hits = 0

2 (inside) to (outside) source dynamic END-USER-NAT DYNAMIC-NAT-POOL

    translate_hits = 15, untranslate_hits = 0
```

STATIC PAT

As streaming servers need to be accessed from outside world, STATIC PAT needs to be configured.

FIREWALL(config)# object network STREAMING-SERVER-1

FIREWALL (config-network-object)# host 192.168.0.1

FIREWALL (config-network-object)# NAT (dmz,outside) static 12.12.12.13 service TCP telnet 8080

Above commands configure static NAT by mapping 192.168.0.1:23 to 12.12.12.13:8080 port. As traffic from low to high-security level is not allowed by default, access list permitting telnet traffic from outside interface needs to be allowed by following commands:

FIREWALL(config)# access-list ALLOW-STREAMING-SERVER1 extended permit TCP any host 192.168.0.1 eq telnet

FIREWALL(config)# interface Ethernet 2

FIREWALL(config-if)# access-group ALLOW-STREAMING-SERVER1 in interface outside

Verification

Telnet 12.12.12.13 8080 from ISP1 router. By static NAT, access of STREAMING-SERVER1 should be successful.

Show xlate/NAT command can be used to verify the above connection.

```
FIREWALL# show xlate

3 in use, 3 most used

Flags: D - DNS, e - extended, I - identity, i - dynamic, r - portmap,
            s - static, T - twice, N - net-to-net

NAT from inside:10.0.0.1 to outside:12.12.12.12

    flags s idle 0:13:38 timeout 0:00:00

TCP PAT from DMZ:192.168.0.1 23-23 to outside:12.12.12.13 8080-8080

    flags sr idle 0:00:15 timeout 0:00:00

NAT from inside:172.16.0.1 to outside:12.12.12.6 flags i idle 0:10:41 timeout 3:00:00
```

```
FIREWALL# Show NAT

Auto NAT Policies (Section 2)

1 (inside) to (outside) source static MANAGEMENT-STATION 12.12.12.12

    translate_hits = 7, untranslate_hits = 0

2 (DMZ) to (outside) source static STREAMING-SERVER-1 12.12.12.13      service tcp
telnet 8080

    translate_hits = 1, untranslate_hits = 0

3 (inside) to (outside) source dynamic END-USER-NAT DYNAMIC-NAT-POOL

    translate_hits = 15, untranslate_hits = 0
```

Lab 1.3: Implementing Port Security

Dynamic *ARP* inspection helps to mitigate the common attack of *ARP* spoofing in which an attacker tries to reply to *ARP* requests and sends its own *MAC* address, which results in man-in-the-middle attacks. All such kind of attacks happen after connecting the malicious device to the Switch or Router. Port Security is used to bind the MAC address of known devices to the physical ports and violation action is also defined. Therefore, if an attacker tries to connect its PC or embedded device to the switch port, then it will shut down or restrict the attacker from even generating an attack.

In this lab, SW1 and SW2 will be configured for port security. Same concept can be applied on switching segments of remote office.

In order to implement the concept of port security. The MAC address of PCs representing the End-User's LAN and router representing the management station is noted.
MAC Address to be bound on SW1 switch port Ethernet 0/1: c203.19ac.0000
MAC Address to be bound on SW2 switch port Ethernet 0/2: 0050.7966.6801
MAC Address to be bound on SW2 switch port Ethernet 0/1: 0050.7966.6802
MAC address to be bound on SW1's Ethernet 0/1 is a management station simulated by router. This mac address will be changed from CLI to verify effect of port security and its violation.

SW1
In order to implement port security, following commands are used:
SW1(config)# interface ethernet 0/1
SW1(config-if)#switchport mode access
SW1(config-if)# switchport port-security mac-address sticky
SW1(config-if)# switchport port-security maximum 1
SW1(config-if)# switchport port-security violation shutdown
SW1(config-if)# switchport port-security

SW2
SW2(config)# interface ethernet 0/2

Verification
Following command is used to verify the port security status of a port along with violation action:
SW1#sho port-security interface ethernet 0/1
SW2(config-if)#switchport mode access
SW2(config-if)# switchport port-security mac-address sticky

SW2(config-if)# switchport port-security maximum 1

SW2(config-if)# switchport port-security violation shutdown

SW2(config-if)# switchport port-security

SW2(config)# interface ethernet 0/1

SW2(config-if)#switchport mode access

SW2(config-if)# switchport port-security mac-address sticky

SW2(config-if)# switchport port-security maximum 1

SW2(config-if)# switchport port-security violation shutdown

SW2(config-if)# switchport port-security

Above commands show how to bind a single MAC address on specific port along with violation action if someone with some other MAC address tries to connect to same port. switchport port-security maximum 1 allows only one mac address statically defined by switchport port-security mac-address <MAC-ADDRESS> command. After defining the port-security main parameters, switchport port-security command need to be configured on port for port security to start working.

```
SW1#show port-security interface eth 0/1
Port Security              : Enabled
Port Status                : Secure-up
Violation Mode             : Shutdown
Aging Time                 : 0 mins
Aging Type                 : Absolute
SecureStatic Address Aging : Disabled
Maximum MAC Addresses      : 1
Total MAC Addresses        : 1
Configured MAC Addresses   : 0
Sticky MAC Addresses       : 1
Last Source Address:Vlan   : 5000.0003.0000:1
Security Violation Count   : 0

SW1#
```

Now change the MAC address of router's port connected to Switch interface Ethernet 0/1 by following commands and then check the status of Ethernet 0/1 on SW1.

R1

R1#conf t

R1 (config)#int fastEthernet 0/0

R1 (config-if)# shutdown

R1 (config-if)#mac-address AAAA.BBBB.CCCC

R1 (config-if)# no shutdown

SW1

SW1#show port-security interface ethernet 0/1

Port Security	: Enabled
Port Status	: Secure-shutdown
Violation Mode	: Shutdown
Aging Time	: 0 mins
Aging Type	: Absolute
SecureStatic Address Aging	: Disabled
Maximum MAC Addresses	: 1
Total MAC Addresses	: 1
Configured MAC Addresses	: 1
Sticky MAC Addresses	: 0
Last Source Address:Vlan	: aaaa.bbbb.cccc:1
Security Violation Count	: 1

In order to restore the port to secure up, restore the MAC address of port to default value and enter *shutdown* command followed by *no shutdown* command on SW1 port.

R1#conf t

R1 (config)#int fastEthernet 0/0

R1 (config-if)# shutdown

R1 (config-if)#mac-address c203.19ac.0000

> R1 (config-if)# no shutdown
>
> **SW1**
>
> SW1(config)#interface ethernet 0/1
>
> SW1(config-if)#shutdown
>
> SW1(config-if)#no shutdown
>
> ```
> *Dec 31 12:10:33.664: %LINEPROTO-5-UPDOWN: Line protocol on Interface Ethernet0/1,
> changed state to up
> ```
>
> SW1#ping 10.0.0.1
>
> Type escape sequence to abort.
>
> ```
> Sending 5, 100-byte ICMP Echos to 10.0.0.1, timeout is 2 seconds:
> ```
>
> ```
> .!!!!
> ```
>
> ```
> Success rate is 80 percent (4/5), round-trip min/avg/max = 9/10/11 ms
> ```

Lab 1.4: Protecting the Network Infrastructure from rogue DHCP Server by Implementing DHCP SNOOPING Feature

In this lab, main focus is to protect the official DHCP server of corporate offices. IP DHCP Snooping feature helps in protecting clients from getting IP address from rogue DHCP server being set up by an attacker or disgruntled employee.

SW2
In order to implement DHCP Snooping, the following command is executed first:
SW2#configure terminal
SW2(config)# IP dhcp snooping
As the security of clients in different VLANs is the major concern, following command is used to enable it for different VLANs.
SW2(config)# IP dhcp snooping VLAN 1
As only one VLAN is used in our scenario, so DHCP Snooping is enabled for VLAN 1.

Next, a switch port, which is connected to corporate DHCP server is declared as trusted ! port for DHCP communication by using following command:

SW2(config)# interface Ethernet 0/3

SW2(config-if)# IP dhcp snooping trust

Similarly, another kind of DHCP attack known as DHCP starvation may result in hammering of DHCP server with IP requests so that DHCP pool becomes fully utilized. In order to prevent that, it is a good idea to rate limit ports other than trusted ports by using the following command:

SW2(config)# interface Ethernet 1/0

SW2(config-if)# IP dhcp snooping limit rate 25

Above command shows that rate limit of 25 packets per second is applied on the switch ! port of rogue DHCP server.

Verification

In order to verify that DHCP Snooping is actually working, shut down the port of corporate DHCP server, start rogue DHCP server and then restart one of the PC representing the End-User's LAN segment. The DORA process will not be completed and client will eventually use APIPA addressing rather than accepting IP from rogue DHCP Server.

Access Console of VPCS and use IP DHCP command for getting IP from DHCP server.

```
PC1
VPCS> ip dhcp
DDD
Can't find dhcp server

VPCS> ip dhcp
DDD
Can't find dhcp server

VPCS> ip dhcp
DDD
Can't find dhcp server

VPCS>
```

Show IP DHCP Snooping command can be used to see the trusted and untrusted ports

SW2#show IP DHCP Snooping

```
Switch DHCP snooping is enabled

Switch DHCP gleaning is disabled

DHCP snooping is configured on following VLANs:

1

DHCP snooping is operational on following VLANs:

1

DHCP snooping is configured on the following L3 Interfaces:

Insertion of option 82 is enabled

    circuit-id default format: VLAN-mod-port

    remote-id: aabb.cc00.0500 (MAC)
```

```
Option 82 on untrusted port is not allowed

Verification of hwaddr field is enabled

Verification of giaddr field is enabled

DHCP snooping trust/rate is configured on the following Interfaces:


Interface              Trusted     Allow option    Rate limit (pps)
---------------------  -------     ------------    ----------------
Ethernet0/3            yes         yes             unlimited
  Custom circuit-ids:
Ethernet1/0            no          no              25
  Custom circuit-ids:
```

Similarly, **show IP dhcp snooping binding** command can be used to display clients list with legitimate IP addresses assigned to them.

SW2#

SW2#show IP dhcp snooping binding

```
MacAddress         IpAddress         Lease(sec)   Type           VLAN  Interface
-----------------  ----------------  ----------   -------------  ----  ---------------
-----
00:50:79:66:68:01  172.16.0.2        86326        dhcp-snooping  1     Ethernet0/2
```

```
00:50:79:66:68:02    172.16.0.1         86318       dhcp-snooping    1       Ethernet0/1
Total number of bindings: 2
```

Lab 1.5: Implementing NAT/PAT Types on Cisco IOS

Just like Lab 1.2, NAT/PAT will be implemented in this lab on Cisco IOS.

Static NAT
Before implementing Static NAT for management and LAN of Remote Office, let us ping simulated internet (210.56.0.1) from Remote LAN nodes (172.16.0.1). As internet router does not have routes for inside networks, it will not be able to route packets destined for 172.16.0.0/24 networks. *debug IP packets* command on ISP2 router will show the following results:

ISP2#debug IP packet

```
*Mar     1  00:06:56.043:   IP:     s=172.16.0.1    (FastEthernet0/0),    d=210.56.0.1
(FastEthernet0/0), len 84, rcvd 3
```

```
*Mar   1 00:06:56.043: IP: s=210.56.0.1 (local), d=172.16.0.1, len 84, unroutable
```

```
*Mar    1 00:06:58.039: IP: tableid=0, s=172.16.0.1 (FastEthernet0/0), d=210.56.0.1
(FastEthernet0/0), routed via RIB
```

```
*Mar     1   00:06:58.039:    IP:    s=172.16.0.1    (FastEthernet0/0),    d=210.56.0.1
(FastEthernet0/0), len 84, rcvd 3
```

```
*Mar   1 00:06:58.043: IP: s=210.56.0.1 (local), d=172.16.0.1, len 84, unroutable
```

```
*Mar    1 00:07:00.023: IP: tableid=0, s=172.16.0.1 (FastEthernet0/0), d=210.56.0.1
(FastEthernet0/0), routed via RIB
```

```
*Mar     1   00:07:00.023:    IP:    s=172.16.0.1    (FastEthernet0/0),    d=210.56.0.1
(FastEthernet0/0), len 84, rcvd 3
```

```
*Mar   1 00:07:00.027: IP: s=210.56.0.1 (local), d=172.16.0.1, len 84, unroutable
```

To work around this problem, Static NAT for management PC will be implemented.

R2(config)#IP NAT inside source static 172.16.0.252 13.13.13.13

R2(config)#interface FastEthernet 0/1

R2(config-if)#IP NAT inside

R2(config)#interface FastEthernet 0/0

R2(config-if)#IP NAT outside

Ping 210.56.0.1 from management station again. This time ISP1 will send reply as 13.13.13.13 will be used as source address from R2, which is also advertised in Simulated Internet.

VPCS> ping 210.56.0.1

```
PC2                                                    —   □   ×

VPCS> ping 210.56.0.1

84 bytes from 210.56.0.1 icmp_seq=1 ttl=254 time=21.632 ms
84 bytes from 210.56.0.1 icmp_seq=2 ttl=254 time=16.645 ms
84 bytes from 210.56.0.1 icmp_seq=3 ttl=254 time=15.438 ms
84 bytes from 210.56.0.1 icmp_seq=4 ttl=254 time=18.846 ms
84 bytes from 210.56.0.1 icmp_seq=5 ttl=254 time=18.985 ms

VPCS>
```

IP packet debugging is on.

```
ISP2                                                   —   □   ×

ISP2(config)#end
ISP2#debi
ISP2#debi
*Mar  1 00:04:27.079: %SYS-5-CONFIG_I: Configured from console by consolu
ISP2#debug ip pa
ISP2#debug ip packet
IP packet debugging is on
ISP2#
*Mar  1 00:04:37.059: IP: tableid=0, s=13.13.13.13 (FastEthernet0/0), d=210.56.0
.1 (FastEthernet0/0), routed via RIB
*Mar  1 00:04:37.059: IP: s=13.13.13.13 (FastEthernet0/0), d=210.56.0.1 (FastEth
ernet0/0), len 84, rcvd 3
*Mar  1 00:04:37.063: IP: tableid=0, s=210.56.0.1 (local), d=13.13.13.13 (FastEt
hernet0/0), routed via FIB
*Mar  1 00:04:37.063: IP: s=210.56.0.1 (local), d=13.13.13.13 (FastEthernet0/0),
 len 84, sending
*Mar  1 00:04:38.079: IP: tableid=0, s=13.13.13.13 (FastEthernet0/0), d=210.56.0
.1 (FastEthernet0/0), routed via RIB
*Mar  1 00:04:38.079: IP: s=13.13.13.13 (FastEthernet0/0), d=210.56.0.1 (FastEth
ernet0/0), len 84, rcvd 3
*Mar  1 00:04:38.083: IP: tableid=0, s=210.56.0.1 (local), d=13.13.13.13 (FastEt
hernet0/0), routed via FIB
*Mar  1 00:04:38.083: IP: s=210.56.0.1 (local), d=13.13.13.13 (FastEthernet0/0),
 len 84, sending
```

Dynamic NAT

In order to perform Dynamic NAT, publically routable IP pool is required. Let us say that pool is 13.13.13.0/29. It means six IP addresses can be used from this pool. Let us use this pool for Remote Office End-users LAN.

R2(config)#IP NAT pool REMOTE-LAN-POOL 13.13.13.1 13.13.13.6 netmask 255.255.255.248

> The above commands create a range of IP addresses, which will be used as source IP for End-User LAN PCs.
>
> R2(config)# IP access-list standard REMOTE-LAN-USERS
>
> R2(config-std-nacl)#permit 172.16.0.0 0.0.0.255
>
> R2(config)#IP NAT inside source list REMOTE-LAN-USERS pool REMOTE-LAN-POOL
>
> Above commands create Nat rule for 172.16.0.0/24 subnet with dynamic NAT by using REMOTE-LAN-POOL defined above. Remote LAN users are matched by using named standard access-list.

Verification

In order to verify Dynamic NAT, ping 210.56.0.1 from END-USER LAN, as public IP pool is advertised in simulated internet LAN, and it will be used in source IP address field END-USER LAN should be able to get PING results as shown below:

VPCS> ping 210.56.0.1

```
PC1                                                    —   □   ×

VPCS> ping 210.56.0.1

84 bytes from 210.56.0.1 icmp_seq=1 ttl=254 time=44.693 ms
84 bytes from 210.56.0.1 icmp_seq=2 ttl=254 time=16.244 ms
84 bytes from 210.56.0.1 icmp_seq=3 ttl=254 time=15.578 ms
84 bytes from 210.56.0.1 icmp_seq=4 ttl=254 time=17.188 ms
84 bytes from 210.56.0.1 icmp_seq=5 ttl=254 time=27.872 ms

VPCS>
```

Similarly, show IP NAT translations command can be used on R2 to see current translations.

R2#show IP NAT translations

```
Pro     Inside global     Inside local      Outside local     Outside global
---     13.13.13.1        172.16.0.1        ---               ---
---     13.13.13.13       172.16.0.252      ---               ---
```

R2#

Similarly, show IP NAT statistics command can be used to see the NAT statistics like total translated packets, inside/outside interfaces, etc.

R2#show IP NAT statistics

```
R2                                                          —    □    ✕

R2(config)#end
R2#do
*Mar  1 00:17:24.655: %SYS-5-CONFIG_I: Configured from console by consoshow ip n
a
R2#show ip nat st
R2#show ip nat statistics
Total active translations: 2 (1 static, 1 dynamic; 0 extended)
Outside interfaces:
  FastEthernet0/0
Inside interfaces:
  FastEthernet0/1
Hits: 35  Misses: 0
CEF Translated packets: 35, CEF Punted packets: 0
Expired translations: 20
Dynamic mappings:
-- Inside Source
[Id: 1] access-list REMOTE-LAN-USERS pool REMOTE-LAN-POOL refcount 1
 pool REMOTE-LAN-POOL: netmask 255.255.255.248
        start 13.13.13.1 end 13.13.13.6
        type generic, total addresses 6, allocated 1 (16%), misses 0
Appl doors: 0
Normal doors: 0
Queued Packets: 0
R2#
```

Similarly, show IP access-list command can also be used to verify either traffic being matched by ACL used in NAT instance.

R2#sho IP access-lists

```
Standard IP access list REMOTE-LAN-USERS
    10 permit 172.16.0.0, wildcard bits 0.0.0.255 (1 match)
```

STATIC PAT

As streaming servers need to be accessed from outside world, STATIC PAT needs to be configured.

R2(config)#IP NAT inside source static tcp 192.168.0.1 23 13.13.13.14 9090

R2(config)#interface FastEthernet 1/0

R2(config-if)#IP NAT inside

Above commands configure static NAT by mapping 192.168.0.1:23 to 13.13.13.14:9090 port. Whenever 13.13.13.14:9090 is accessed, it will provide telnet session of Streaming Server- 1 of Remote office.

Verification

Telnet 13.13.13.14 9090 from ISP2 router. By static PAT, access of STREAMING-SERVER1 should be successful.

ISP2#telnet 13.13.13.14 9090

```
Trying 13.13.13.14, 9090 ... Open
```

Remote-Streaming-Server-1#

R2#show IP NAT translations

```
Pro    Inside global        Inside local         Outside local        Outside global
---    13.13.13.1           172.16.0.1           ---                  ---
---    13.13.13.13          172.16.0.252         ---                  ---
tcp    13.13.13.14:9090     192.168.0.1:23  210.56.0.1:21765          210.56.0.1:21765
tcp    13.13.13.14:9090     192.168.0.1:23  ---                       ---
```

DYNAMIC PAT

Configuration of Dynamic PAT is almost same as Dynamic NAT. By adding keyword "overload" at the end of Dynamic NAT statement used above, R2 will implement the Dynamic PAT.

R2(config)#IP NAT inside source list REMOTE-LAN-USERS pool REMOTE-LAN-POOL overload

Chapter 2: Cisco Security Devices GUI and Secured CLI Management

Technology Brief

In this chapter, we will continue to explore the new methodologies by which we can increase the security of networking devices. In the past, Command Line Interface (CLI) used to be the main method by which Cisco devices can be configured to operate in production environment. However, with upcoming versions of IOS, Cisco has improved the Graphical User Interface (GUI) of its devices to some extent.

Before moving to different methods of securing graphical management access of network devices, first, we need to categorize our network infrastructure, and then implement the correct security measures to build best possible security solution.

Consider an analogy of buying some used vehicle or electronic component. If a single core component of that purchased item is not working well, e.g., transmission engine, etc., then the whole vehicle would be useless. Same principle applies on computer networks. If network administrator applies access filter on CLI as per best practices but forgets to apply it on HTTP/HTTPS interface of device, then the whole paradigm of network security will be of no use.

Basic Elements of Network Infrastructure: A network infrastructure can be divided into three basic elements or functions namely:

- **Management Function/Plane:** Whenever a network administrator tries to access a networking device or a console of some server, any kind of traffic and supporting protocols used to access the device will lie in this category. For example, using Telnet, SSH or console port to access router or switch, etc. Similarly, when we use SNMP, Syslog, NTP to get information related to different nodes on a network, it is also a part of management plane

- **Control Function/Plane:** Inside control function/plane lies any kind of traffic, which requires some kind of processing usage of networking device. We know that every networking device has some embedded processing unit, which is required to perform everything from calculating best routes in the network to the filtering of data and many more. Examples include CPU usage by routing protocols. Similarly, any kind of traffic that is directed for networking device itself, etc.

- **Data Function/Plane:** It includes any kind of traffic moving physically between networking devices. For example, traffic from a host of one network to the host of the

same or some other network. Therefore, it includes any kind of traffic that has to leave the networking device and move over the physical medium as well.

Table 13 summarizes the above concept and mitigation against risks and vulnerabilities involved in each plane.

Name	Purpose	Examples	Mitigating Common Attacks
Management Plane	Allow network administrators to access networking devices	SSH/Telnet sessions with router/switch, Syslog messages, SNMP traps and get messages, etc.	Use of encrypted protocols like SSH/SFTP instead of TELNET/TFTP. Role-based access control, Secure NTP, Login restrictions, AAA
Control Plane	Any kind of traffic, which requires device-processing power	Routing Protocols path calculation and their updates. Traffic directed to the IP address of device itself	Use of authentication feature in routing protocols. Using different control plane features present in specific models of device
Data Plane	Physical movement of data among networking devices	Any kind of traffic movement between hosts	Use of ACLS, STP safeguards, Port Security, Firewalls, IDS / IPS for security

Table 13- Categorization of Traffic Generated in a Network

It is always suggested to implement the already made best security practices, which if implemented correctly, increases the security posture of the network. Some of them are:

Strong Password Recommendations: It is one of the significant security practices to implement strong passwords wherever required. Password should not include some word or sentence easily guessable by victim's personality or background. Minimum length as suggested by different standards must be implemented and must include different character types like "P@ssw@rd:10". In this string, different characters make it difficult to break although it sounds like a password keyword. Attackers always try to break password by two common password attacks namely *dictionary* and *brute force attacks*. In dictionary attacks, login process is automated using a list of guessable and daily life words. Words keep changing unless correct password is detected. In brute force attacks, instead of using

list of words, a combination of characters is used as input to password field. This string keeps incrementing in length to get to the correct password. By using long and complex password, we can increase the time to insanely indefinite length before brute force attack can guess our password.

Lockout after Login Failure: We can also set the maximum login attempts within specific time interval. After those attempts, we can lock the login process for specific time. This method can slow down different attacks like brute force as explained earlier.

User Authentication: Whenever a network administrator requires accessing an asset of an organization, username/password combination must be used instead of password. By assigning and using different usernames, and then proper auditing it using AAA (explained later), we will know which user tried to break-in at the hour of need.

Role Based Access Control (RBAC): Let us say in an organization, the IT department comprises of ten employees. Suppose, only two of them, i.e., Chris and John maintain and change the configuration of networking devices like routers, switches, and firewalls while remaining others are assigned to some specific tasks like *help-desk, network support, IT support,* etc. If anyone other than Chris and John who need specific access of commands but have level 15 access and accidentally erases something like IP addresses from interfaces or even erase flash as well as start-up configuration file, then it would be very difficult to trace the culprit. Therefore, by implementing RBAC, we set custom privilege levels and assign them to different users and groups depending on their need. Since it is a known fact that as we log in a router or other Cisco devices, we get to the user mode or privilege level 1 and is denoted as '>'. We enter into level 15, which is highest level of access in Cisco devices, by entering *enable* and then entering password for it. We can set custom privilege levels in between 1 and 15. Anyone with level 4, would have access to everything below it. To understand it, consider yourself sitting at the top of mountain, what will you see? Almost everything below, same applies to custom privileges.

Parser Views: Another great feature in Cisco devices is parser views. Parser views do the same thing as custom privilege levels but they have fewer commands, and they give a cleaner configuration view. From implementation point of view, first, we define a view and then assign a user or group and commands to it.

Encrypted Protocols for Remote Access: Either using *in-band* or *out-of-band* management, first priority should be to use encrypted protocols such as SSH instead of TELNET. We may be trying to prevent our network from public attacks, but attacker may be some disgruntled employee who has installed *Wireshark* on local PC and sniff the traffic to launch attack from local network. It is then merely a child's play these days to follow TCP/UDP streams within *Wireshark* software to see what is going on. In case there

is a legacy device, which does not have SSH support then VPN tunnel should be used where possible.

Logging: Logging not only helps in auditing the network and system administrators about their activities on network infrastructure but also helps in viewing the system events that may be generated by networking devices like routers, switches or firewalls, etc. that may occur due to some failure or surpassing certain threshold like CPU or RAM usage is exceeded. Now there are different levels of log generated by these devices.

As far as Cisco devices and Cisco IOS are concerned, they can send log output to following destinations:

- **Console:** A Router/Switch/Firewall can send log messages to the connected terminal. For example, an attached computer with terminal emulation program running like HyperTerminal
- **VTY Lines:** Whenever an administrator tries to remotely connect to Cisco devices, a *VTY line* gets activated for that *exec session*. Depending on device model, this number may vary. Terminal Monitor command also needs to be issued at privilege level 15 to see the logs on terminal
- **Buffer:** In order to save log messages for later analysis, device's internal memory (RAM) can be used. Depending on the size of RAM dedicated for storing log messages, which is named as buffer. These messages are stored on first-in/first-out basis. As RAM gets empty on reboot, so is the buffer
- **SNMP Server:** Log messages can be sent to the SNMP server in the form of SNMP TRAPs if configured on devices. Normally SNMPv3 is preferred due to its support for Hashing and Encryption
- **Syslog Server:** A Syslog server is a dedicated device, whose purpose is to store any kind of log messages directed to it. Depending on the nature of event, which generates a log message, an immediate action may be required by responsible person otherwise situation may get worse. To categorize the events, Syslog uses eight severity levels from zero to seven as in Table 14, with zero being more critical one when system becomes severely degraded.

Name	Severity Level	Description
Emergencies	0	System is Unusable
Alerts	1	Immediate Action Needed
Critical	2	Critical Condition
Errors	3	Error Condition
Warnings	4	Warning Condition
Notifications	5	Normal but Require Attention
Informational	6	Informational messages
Debugging	7	Debugging messages with maximum details depending on number of processes for which debugging is enabled

Table 14- Syslog Severity Levels and their Descriptions

A Syslog being most feasible option is based on client-server architecture. It means there will be a Syslog server and multiple Syslog Clients (different networking devices). Keep it in mind that more detailed log messages will require more hard drive space for storage. Normally a RAID technology is also considered where log belongs to an important infrastructure.

Since log messages contain sensitive information leakage of which may result in very serious attacks on network. The payload of Syslog messages may contain information like IP addresses, username/password of logged in users, etc. It should be encrypted when in transit over the network.

Management Tools for Cisco Devices and Appliances

It would have been great if single software could be used to manage and monitor every single product from Cisco. Unfortunately, multiple management tools are used in conjunction to perform the overall best practices related to management and monitoring of Cisco devices.

Table 15 summarizes the top Cisco management tools:

Management Tool Name	Description
Adaptive Security Device Manager (ASDM)	Used to manage Cisco ASA firewall series via Graphical User Interface (GUI). It is one to one management software, i.e., only one device can be configured at a time
Configuration Professional (CCP)	Used for GUI based management of Cisco routers and switches. Although multiple devices can be discovered and added in CCP, only one device can be configured at a time
IPS Device Manager (IDM)	Used to manage standalone IPS appliance or IPS module in ASA firewall
IPS Manager Express(IME)	Multiple IPS sensors can be added in IME, but only one sensor can be configured at a time
Cisco Security Manager (CSM)	CSM can manage Cisco routers, switches, IPS sensors and ASA firewall series. Although it can be considered as a single place to manage everything on a network segment as it has ability to push policies to multiple devices at a time, but it has its own limitations. For example, CSM does not support ASA next-generation firewall series (5500-CX series)
Cisco Prime Infrastructure & Cisco Prime Security Manager (PRSM)	Apart from CSM functionality, Cisco Prime Infrastructure also supports Wireless LAN Controllers (WLC). One major advantage over CSM is support for 5500-CX series firewalls
Identity Services Engine (ISE)	Acts as a single policy control point for entire enterprise including wired and wireless technologies. Before giving access to endpoints or even networking devices itself, ISE checks their identity, location, time, type of device, and even health of endpoints to make sure that they comply with company's policy like antivirus, latest service pack and OS updates, etc. Most of the time people prefer ACS over ISE, although ISE can implement AAA, but it is not a complete replacement of ACS
Access Control Server (ACS)	Any network device that wishes to implement AAA becomes client of this server, which contains usernames passwords and associated level of authorization with each username.

	Two protocols are commonly used in communication between client and ACS server namely TACACS+ and RADIUS. Generally, TACACS+ is used for communication between client device and server for giving access to network administrator. Similarly, RADIUS is normally preferred as protocol between device and ACS server for allowing access to end-users of the network

Table 15- Cisco Management Tools and their Descriptions

Cisco Prime Infrastructure

As explained in Table 15, CPI provides network administrators a single interface for provisioning, monitoring and troubleshooting both wired (Routers/Switches/ASA, etc.) and wireless (Wireless LAN Controllers etc.) devices.

Unlike ASDM/CCP, which allows to configure and monitor one device at a time, Cisco Prime allows to configure and monitor multiple Wireless LAN Controllers (WLC) and switches at a time. Prime Infrastructure also provides graphical view of multiple controllers and access points, which reduce the factor of human error from configuration perspective. SNMP, which is the industry standard protocol, is used for communication between networking devices and Cisco Prime Infrastructure.

The following are the supported WLC by Prime Infrastructure:

- Cisco 2106 Wireless LAN Controllers
- Cisco 2500 Series Wireless Controllers
- Cisco 4400 Series Wireless LAN Controllers
- Cisco 5508 Series Wireless Controllers
- Cisco Wireless Services Modules (WiSMs) for Cisco Catalyst 6500 Series Switches
- Cisco Wireless Services Module 2 (WiSM2) for Cisco Catalyst 6500 Series Switches
- Cisco Flex 7500 Series Wireless Controllers
- Cisco Flex 8500 Series Wireless Controllers
- Cisco Grey Nicols Wireless Controllers
- Cisco Virtual Wireless Controllers

The following access points are supported in Prime Infrastructure:

- Cisco Aironet 801, 802, 1040, 1100, 1130, 1140, 1200, 1230, 1240, 1250, 1260, 1310, 1500, 1522, 1524, 1552, 2600i, 2600e, 3500i, 3500e, 3500p, 3600i, and 3600e Series Lightweight Access Points
- Cisco Aironet 1040, 1100, 1130, 1141, 1142, 1200, 1240, 1250, 1260, 2600i, and 2600e Autonomous Access Points
- Cisco 600 Series OfficeExtend Access Points
- Cisco Aironet Access Points running Lightweight Access Point Protocol (LWAPP) or Control and Provisioning of Wireless Access Points (CAPWAP) protocol

Cisco Security Manager (CSM)

Although CSM can be used as single interface for managing Cisco devices ranging from switches, routers to ASA and IPS appliances, Cisco Security Manager provides a comprehensive management solution for:

- Cisco ASA 5500 Series Adaptive Security Appliances
- Cisco intrusion prevention systems 4200 and 4500 Series Sensors
- Cisco AnyConnect Secure Mobility Client

Benefit of using CSM in Corporate Environment

Policy and Object Management: Unlike ASDM/CCP, CSM facilitates the network administrators to define a policy objects and push that policy to multiple devices at a time, which saves time and reduces human error in deployment phase.

Event Management: Having support for Syslog messages generated by networking devices, CSM provides the bird's eye view over the whole network topology of network with its real-time event viewing system. With customizable views for firewalls, IPS sensors, and other devices, CSM helps network administrators to correlate different security events happening in overall network design.

Reporting and Troubleshooting: Just like ASDM/CCP, CSM also has nice troubleshooting tools like *Ping, Traceroute* and *Packet Tracer*. Similarly, reporting feature allows export or E-mail delivery of reports in CSV/PDF format.

Health and Performance Monitoring (HPM): HPM helps in monitoring the health and other performance parameters of firewall and other devices. Custom thresholds levels can also be defined for various parameters that provide alerts whenever a certain threshold is crossed.

Talos Security Intelligence Research Group Support: One of the major advantages of using CSM in production environment is getting recommendations and support from Talos Security Intelligence Research Group of Cisco, which helps network administrators to tune their security signatures as per their network design.

Case Study

In this section, case study from last chapter will be used as this chapter introduced some new methodologies of networking device hardening by GUI tools.

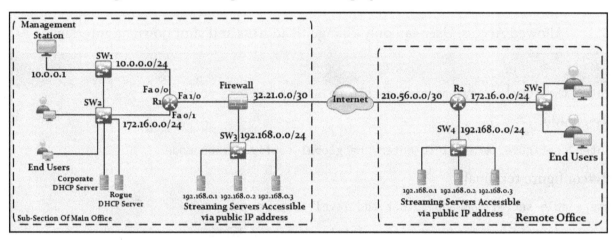

Figure 19- Security Devices GUI and Secure CLI Management Case Study

Lab 2.1: Implementation of RBAC via Custom Privilege Levels Using CLI

Cisco IOS allows users to make different privilege levels from Level 1 to Level 15; it eases the management of network staff itself. Level 15 access is a great concern regarding the security of device. Any user with level 15 access can do anything on Cisco routers and switches. To overcome this problem, the concept of least privilege must be implemented, which states that a user should be provided with as limited access as possible while making sure that the tasks assigned to that user can be performed with that limited access.

Another method of implementing the above concept is using parser views. Although, parser views give cleaner look and understanding as compared to custom privilege levels but it is rarely used. Parser views limit the view or number of commands irrespective of privilege level.

In this lab, following two users will be created with respective access limitations defined below:

Username1: IPSpecialist

Password: P@$$word:10

Privilege level: 15

Username2: NetworkSupport

Password: Network$upport:10

Privilege level 4

Allowed Access: User can only change IP address and shut down an interfaces.

R1:
Enter the level 15 by entering enable on user privilege mode
R1>enable
Enter configure terminal to enter the global configuration mode
R1#configure terminal
Use enable secret command to set the level 15 password
Use long string of password with multiple character types
R1(config)# enable secret 0 P@$$word:10
Define a usernames and passwords with associated privilege level
R1(config)#username IPSpecialist privilege 15 secret 0 P@$$word:10
R1(config)#username NetworkSupport privilege 4 secret 0 Network$upport:10
Now define the commands associated with custom privilege levels
R1(config)#privilege interface level 4 shutdown
R1(config)#privilege interface level 4 IP address
R1(config)#privilege interface level 4 no shutdown
R1(config)#privilege interface level 4 no IP address
R1(config)#privilege configure level 4 interface
R1(config)#privilege exec level 4 configure terminal
R1(config)#privilege exec level 4 configure
Set the hostname of your choice
R1(config)#hostname R1

```
Set the domain name for SSH to work
```

R1(config)#IP domain name IPSpecialist.net

R1(config)#crypto key generate rsa general-keys modulus 1024

```
Set the SSH version to 2
```

R1(config)#IP ssh version 2

```
Go to the line console sub configuration mode to set authentication
```

R1(config)#line console 0

R1(config-line)#login local

```
Similarly, go to the line vty sub configuration mode to do the same
```

R1(config)#line vty 0 903

R1(config-line)# login local

```
Enable only SSH. Disable Telnet for being less secure
```

R1(config-line)# transport input ssh

R1(config-line)# Also call access list to limit access to only to management-station

R1(config-line)#access-class MGMT-STATION in

```
Now define MGMT-STATION named based ACL
```

R1(config)#IP access-list standard MGMT-STATION

R1(config-std-nacl)#permit host 10.0.0.1

```
Go to line aux sub-configuration mode
```

R1(config-line)# login local

Verification

In real network, we use multiple stations for network staff. However, in virtual environment, same management station with an IP address of 10.0.0.1 will be used to verify the above concept.

Login to R1 router using putty and SSH as choice of protocol. When asked for username and password prompt use "NetworkSupport" as username and "Network$upport:10" as password to log in.

When a user enters *show run* command, which shows running configuration of router, error will be prompted, as it is not allowed at privilege level 4. Show privilege command can be used to see current privilege level.

```
10.0.0.254 - PuTTY
login as: NetworkSupport
Using keyboard-interactive authentication.
Password:

R1#sho run
        ^
% Invalid input detected at '^' marker.

R1#sho priv
R1#sho privilege
Current privilege level is 4
R1#
```

As IP addressing and interface shutdown commands are allowed at privilege level 4, very few options are available at sub-configuration mode of specific interfaces.

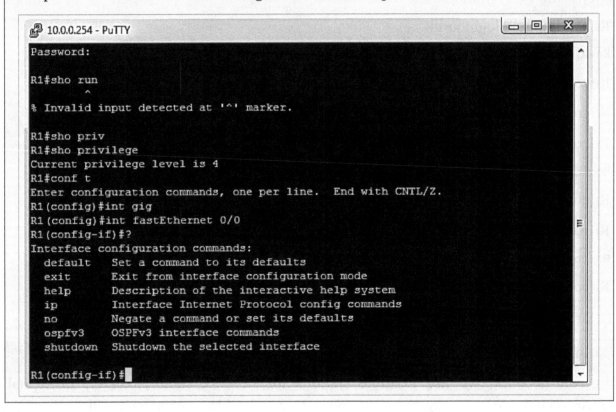

```
10.0.0.254 - PuTTY
Password:

R1#sho run
        ^
% Invalid input detected at '^' marker.

R1#sho priv
R1#sho privilege
Current privilege level is 4
R1#conf t
Enter configuration commands, one per line.  End with CNTL/Z.
R1(config)#int gig
R1(config)#int fastEthernet 0/0
R1(config-if)#?
Interface configuration commands:
  default   Set a command to its defaults
  exit      Exit from interface configuration mode
  help      Description of the interactive help system
  ip        Interface Internet Protocol config commands
  no        Negate a command or set its defaults
  ospfv3    OSPFv3 interface commands
  shutdown  Shutdown the selected interface

R1(config-if)#
```

In the second part of this lab, same task will be performed by using parser view. Following user will be created in the above lab scenario with respective access limitations defined below:

> Username: Chris
>
> Password: P@$$word:10
>
> Privilege level: 15
>
> Associated Parser view: help-desk

Associated set of commands with parser view: Can view *show version, show IP* and *show* commands.

R1:
Parser view requires AAA to be enabled first. Enter "aaa new-model" command.

R1(config)# aaa new-model

R1(config)#! Use enable secret to enter into root view

R1# enable view

Password:

```
Use show parser view command to check current parser view.
```

R1# show parser view

```
Current view is 'root'.
```

```
Create new parser view with name help-desk and enter associated commands.
```

R1#configure terminal

R1(config)# parser view help-desk

R1(config-view)# secret P@$$word:10

R1(config-view)#commands exec include all show IP

R1(config-view)# commands exec include all show version

R1(config-view)# commands exec include show

```
Now, create a username and associated parser view with it.
```

R1(config)#username Chris view help-desk privilege 15 secret P@$$word:10

```
Configure the router to use local database for Authentication and Authorization.
```

R1(config)#aaa authorization exec default local

R1(config)#aaa authentication login default local

> Two method lists are called in the above command. Method list with name "default" gets active on any kind of access. If we define a custom method list, then it must be called on line console and line vty sub configuration.

Verification

Login to router R1 with username "Chris" and associated password. Although, user has privilege level 15 access but limited commands will be displayed as defined in help-desk parser view.

```
10.0.0.254 - PuTTY
login as: Chris
Using keyboard-interactive authentication.
Password:

R1#sho par
R1#sho parser view
Current view is 'help-desk'

R1#sho ?
  bootflash:  display information about bootflash: file system
  disk0:      display information about disk0: file system
  disk1:      display information about disk1: file system
  flash:      display information about flash: file system
  ip          IP information
  parser      Display parser information
  slot0:      display information about slot0: file system
  slot1:      display information about slot1: file system
  version     System hardware and software status

R1#sho
```

As same IOS command exists for Cisco Switches, above concept is also applicable on Cisco L2 devices.

Firewall

Enter the level 15 by entering "Enable" on user privilege mode.

FIREWALL>enable

Password:

Press Enter as no password is set up to this point.

Enter configure terminal to enter the global configuration mode.

FIREWALL #configure terminal

FIREWALL(config)#

Use enable password command to set the level 15 password.

FIREWALL(config)# enable password P@$$word:10 level 15

FIREWALL(config)# enable password Network$upport:10 level 4

Define a username and password with associated privilege level.

FIREWALL(config)# username IPSpecialist password P@$$word:10 privilege 15

FIREWALL(config)# username NetworkSupport password Network$upport:10 privilege 4

In order to assign custom commands to privilege level 4, following steps are are taken.

Enable commands authorization first.

FIREWALL(config)# aaa authorization command LOCAL

Above command uses the local database configured on firewall. Another option would be the implementation of AAA using TACACS+ protocols.

FIREWALL(config)# privilege level 4 command configure

FIREWALL(config)# privilege level 4 mode configure command interface

FIREWALL(config)# privilege level 4 mode interface command IP

FIREWALL(config)# privilege level 4 mode interface command no

FIREWALL(config)# privilege level 4 mode interface command shutdown

FIREWALL(config)# privilege level 4 mode interface command nameif

In order to restrict the remote connections to specific IP address, let us say only 10.0.0.1 can access FIREWALL from interface with name "inside", use the following commands:

FIREWALL(config)# ssh 10.0.0.1 255.255.255.255 inside

Just like routing and switching devices, crypto key needs to be generated for SSH.

FIREWALL(config)# domain-name ipspecialist.net

FIREWALL(config)# crypto key generate rsa general-keys modulus 1024

In the last step, AAA authentication for SSH must be defined. As no TACACS/RADIUS server is used in this lab, so LOCAL AAA settings will be used.

FIREWALL(config)# aaa authentication ssh console LOCAL

Verification

Login to Firewall using putty and SSH as choice of protocol. When asked for username and password prompt use "NetworkSupport" as username and "Network$upport:10" as password to log in.

When a user enters *show run* command, which shows running configuration of firewall, error will be prompted, as it is not allowed at privilege level 4.

```
1.1.1.2 - PuTTY                                                    _ □ ×
login as: NetworkSupport
NetworkSupport@1.1.1.2's password:
Type help or '?' for a list of available commands.
FIREWALL> en
FIREWALL> enable 4
Password: *****************
FIREWALL# sho run
FIREWALL# sho running-config
               ^
ERROR: % Invalid input detected at '^' marker.
ERROR: Command authorization failed
FIREWALL#
```

As IP addressing and interface shutdown commands are allowed at privilege level 4, very few options are available at sub-configuration mode of specific interfaces.

```
1.1.1.2 - PuTTY                                                    _ □ ×
FIREWALL#
FIREWALL# configure terminal
FIREWALL(config)# interface ethernet 3
FIREWALL(config-if)# ?

Interface configuration commands:
  default   Set a command to its defaults
  exit      Exit from interface configuration mode
  ip        Configure the ip address
  nameif    Assign name to interface
  no        Negate a command or set its defaults
  shutdown  Shutdown the selected interface
FIREWALL(config-if)#
```

Lab 2.2: Implementation of RBAC via Custom Privilege Levels Using GUI

In this lab, tasks performed in previous lab will be performed via Cisco Configuration Professional (CCP) and Adaptive Security Device Manager (ASDM).

R1:
Enter the level 15 by entering "Enable" on user privilege mode. R1>enable Use enable secret command to set the level 15 password. Use a long string of password with multiple character types. R1(config)# enable secret 0 P@$$word:10 Define a usernames and passwords with associated privilege level. R1(config)#username IPSpecialist privilege 15 secret 0 P@$$word:10 For GUI access of Cisco Routers/Switches, CCP requires a username with privilege level 15 access. Next step would be to enable HTTP/HTTP access on R1. R1(config)#IP http server R1(config)#IP http secure-server % Generating 1024 bit RSA keys, keys will be non-exportable...[OK] *Mar 1 00:02:50.227: %SSH-5-ENABLED: SSH 1.99 has been enabled *Mar 1 00:02:50.355: %PKI-4-NOAUTOSAVE: Configuration was modified. Issue "write memory" to save new certificate. R1(config)#IP http authentication local Above commands enable http authentication with local database created on device itself. Open The Cisco Configuration Professional (CCP) from management station with Administrator. Create New Community with name IPSpecialist. Use the R1 IP address and username just created above for discovery process.

Select / Manage Community

Enter information for up to 10 devices for the selected community

IPpecialist

	IP Address/Hostname	Username	Password	Connect Securely
1.	10.0.0.254	IPSpecialist	•••••••••	
2.				
3.				
4.				
5.				
6.				
7.				
8.				
9.				
10.				

Discover all devices   OK   Cancel

As discussed earlier, Multiple Routers/Switches can be added in single community but policy push and configuration/monitoring can be done on single device at a time. HTTPS connection in CCP takes a lot of time. As this lab is for demonstration and understanding of concepts, HTTP version will be used, however, in production environment and as per best practices, HTTPS-based connection should be used by ticking the connect securely option.

After clicking [OK] button, click [Discover] button to start discovery process.

After discovery process, select the device and click [Configure] button.

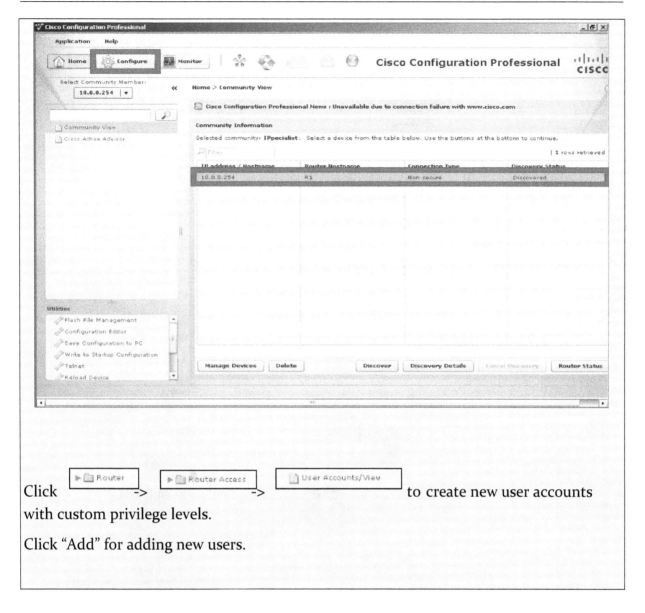

Click -> -> to create new user accounts with custom privilege levels.

Click "Add" for adding new users.

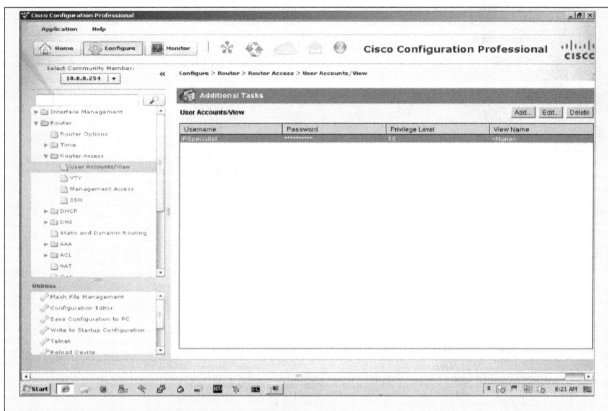

Create NetworkSupport User along with associated privilege level.

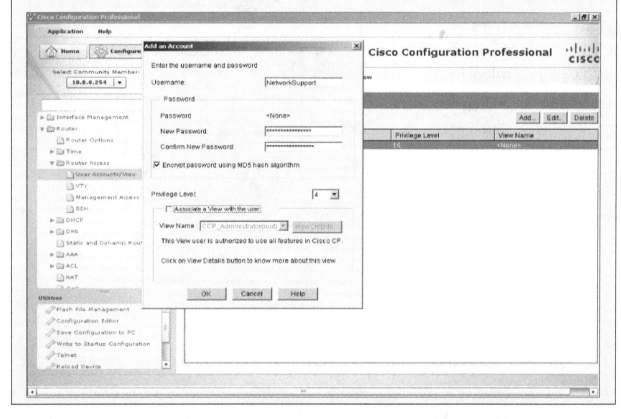

Click "Ok". Next screen will display the CLI commands, which will be sent to Router for creating new username.

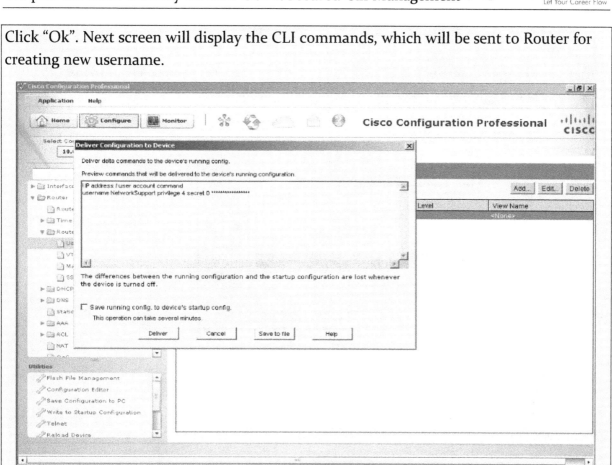

Click "Deliver" to finally create new user.

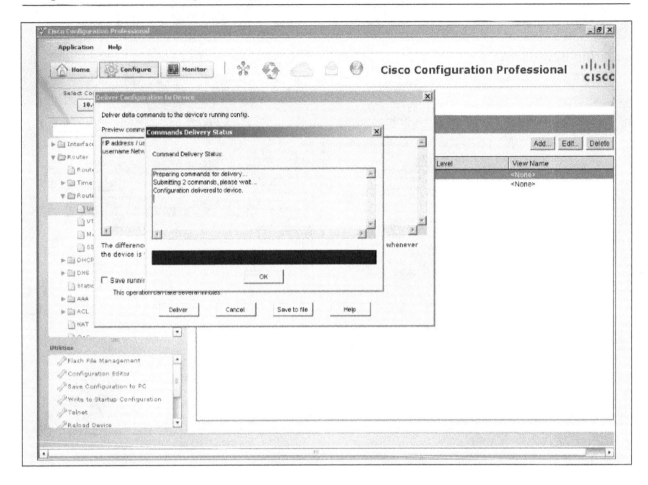

Firewall

In order to access firewall via ASDM, a username with privilege level 15 must be created first.

FIREWALL(config)# username IPSpecialist password P@$$word:10 privilege 15

FIREWALL(config)# http server enable

FIREWALL(config)# http 10.0.0.1 255.255.255.255 inside

FIREWALL(config)# aaa authentication http console LOCAL

FIREWALL(config)# SSL encryption 3des-sha1 aes128-sha1 aes256-sha1 des-sha1

Above commands enable https server for 10.0.0.1 only and uses local database for authentication as AAA is not implemented yet. The last command defines the encryption algorithms for certificate, which will be used in communication with end clients.

Now, open ASDM from Management station and use the above-defined credentials to access it.

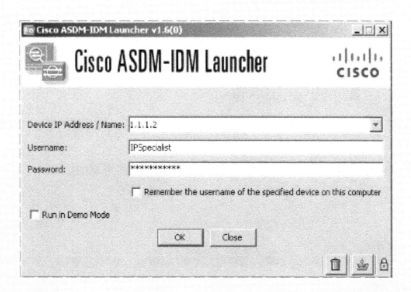

The following dashboard should appear after successful authentication.

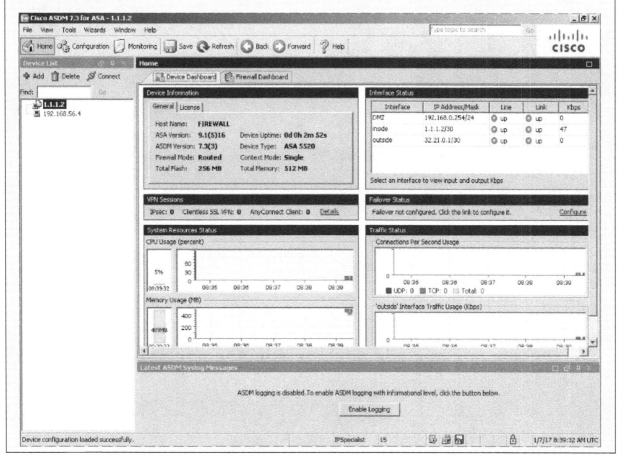

As clear from above figure, most common information like interface IP/status, ASA version etc. is available on dashboard screen.

Click [Configuration] -> [Device Management] -> [Users/AAA] -> [User Accounts] to create new users with custom privilege levels.

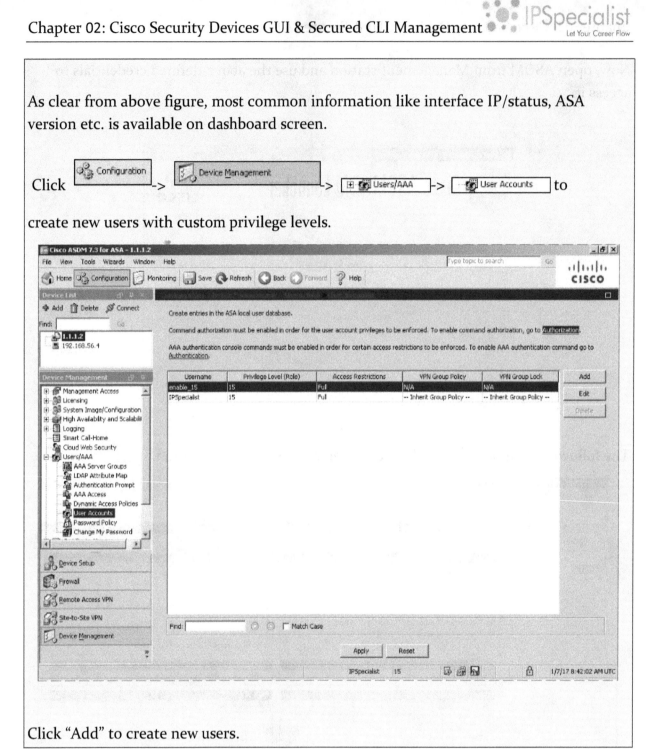

Click "Add" to create new users.

Click "OK".

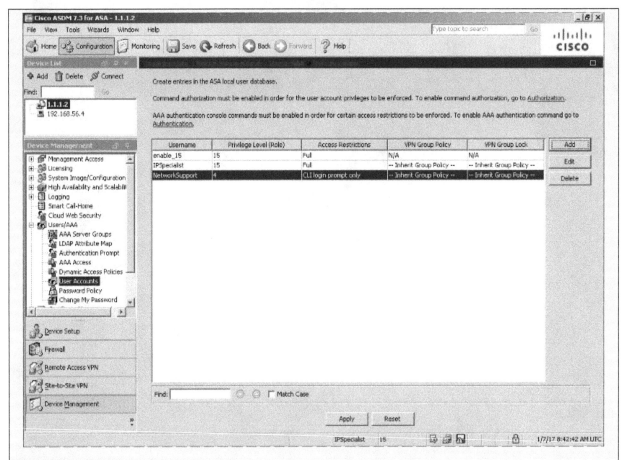

Click "Apply" to send the CLI commands to ASA firewall. Now use putty to check the verification of above created username.

Lab 2.3: Use of SNMPv3 for Secure Network Monitoring

In production environment where tens of thousands of networking devices are used, Network Operation Center (NOC) plays a very critical role. Almost every single vendor supports Simple Network Management Protocol. To configure SNMP, first thing we need is management station, which collects the information regarding different aspects of network devices. Second thing is configuration and software support by networking devices itself. Configuration like type of encryption and hashing running on management station's software must match with SNMP settings on networking devices.

Technically three components are involved in deploying SNMP in a network:

SNMP Manager: It is a software application running on management station to display the collected information from networking devices in a nice and representable manner. Commonly used SNMP software are PRTG, *Solarwinds, OPManager,* etc. Free edition of OPManager will be used in this lab scenario.

SNMP Agent: It is a software running on networking nodes whose different components need to be monitored. Examples include CPU/RAM usage, interface status, etc. UDP port number 161 is used for communication between SNMP agent and SNMP manager.

Management Information Base (MIB): is a collection of information organized hierarchically. These are accessed using a protocol such as SNMP. There are two types of MIBs: *scalar* and *tabular*. Scalar objects define a single object instance whereas, tabular objects define multiple related object instances grouped in MIB tables.

MIBs are collections of definitions, which define the properties of the managed object within the device to be managed.

MIB Example: The typical objects to monitor on a printer are the different cartridge states and maybe the number of printed files, and on a switch, the typical objects of interest are the incoming and outgoing traffic as well as the rate of package loss or the number of packets addressed to a broadcast address.

Table 16 summarizes the features of available SNMP variants:

SNMP version	Features
V1	No Support for encryption and hashing. Plain text community string is used for authentication
V2c	No support for encryption and hashing either. Some great functions like ability to get data in bulk from agents are implemented in version 2c
V3	Support for both encryption (DES) and hashing (MD5 or SHA). Implementation of version 3 has three models. NoAuthNoPriv means no encryption and hashing will be used. AuthNoPriv means only MD5 or SHA based hashing will be used. AuthPriv means both encryption and hashing will be used for SNMP traffic

Table 16- Versions of SNMP and their Features

Another important aspect of collecting information is the time at which that specific event occurs. Attackers may try to change the timestamps setting of router or may introduce rough NTP server in the network to mislead the forensic teams. Thanks to the creators of NTP v3, it has support for authentication with NTP server before considering its time to be the authenticated one.

Although SNMP traps are enough for daily based routing maintenance of network. To have granular control over the events monitoring, Syslog server is used. Open source implementations are widely available for Syslog server. Hits on ACL, login attempts on networking devices along with other features like interfaces status are collected in Syslog server. The only downside of Syslog server is that it generates clear text traffic. If a user enters a login username and password to perform some action, its password will be sent in a clear text to Syslog server. Therefore, encryption needs to be implemented on any kind of Syslog traffic, which includes sensitive information like usernames and passwords.

- It is assumed that previous labs are properly implemented and tested.
- Custom privilege levels, parser views and other concepts implemented in previous labs are also implemented in this lab so that by the end of this section a complete picture of securing management access should be clear and make some sense

---

R1:

Configure remote IP address of SNMP management station with SNMP Engine ID of device.

Use **show SNMP engineID** command to get current EngineID

R1#show SNMP engineID

```
Local SNMP engineID: 800000090300C20648FF0000

Remote Engine ID        IP-addr        Port
```

Now, associate engine ID with IP address of SNMP management station.

R1(config)#snmp-server engineID remote 10.0.0.1 800000090300C20648FF0000

In the second step, a view is created. SNMP with default configuration will send every single piece of information defined in its MIB. If specific information needs to be monitored, then only that information should be included in view. More information regarding MIB hierarchy can be found on Cisco website.

R1(config)# SNMP-server view MyView iso included

ISO sits on the top of MIB hierarchy. We can view everything related to device by just including ISO view in the next step, a Group is created to call a view and specify the action a user can perform with information provided in the view. Apart from collecting information, a user can also change a device configuration by via SNMP.

R1(config)#snmp-server group MyGroup v3 auth read MyView access SNMP-ACL

R1(config)#IP access-list standard SNMP-ACL

R1(config-std-nacl)#permit host 10.0.0.1

R1(config)#! In the above command, MyView has been associated with SNMP-ACL.

Only hosts defined in SNMP-ACL will be able to receive the SNMP Information. Next, a user is created, which will be provided to network administrator to be defined in the SNMP management station software as well.

R1(config)# SNMP-server user MyUser MyGroup v3 auth md5 P@$$word:10

Above command defines a user with name *MyUser* with auth model of SNMP version 3. MD5 is used as algorithm for hashing. Last step is to configure the desired SNMP management station software. In this lab, OP Manager free edition is used.

Same commands can also be configured on Cisco L2 devices as IOS commands of router and switch are same.

Firewall
FIREWALL(config)# snmp-server enable
FIREWALL(config)# snmp-server enable traps all
FIREWALL(config)# snmp-server group MyGroup v3 auth
FIREWALL(config)# snmp-server user MyUser MyGroup v3 auth md5 P@$$word:10
FIREWALL(config)# snmp-server host inside 10.0.0.1 version 3 MyUser
Just like on Cisco IOS, the above commands allow SNMP traps to be received only on management station (10.0.0.1) with AuthNoPriv model of SNMP v3.
SNMP Verification
Click "Manage Engine" pinned to taskbar of provided *VMware* image of *Windows-7*. Following window will open. Click "First Time User" to enter.

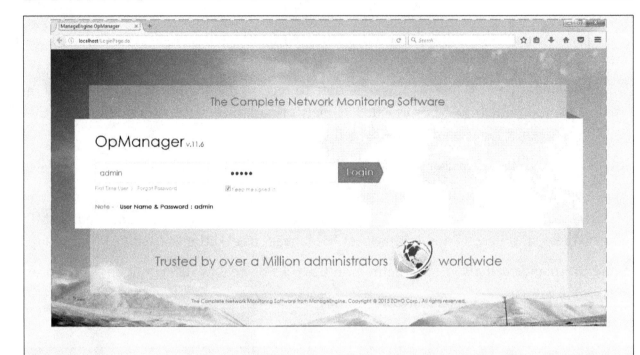

Discovery gives user ability to find devices on IP address range defined by user. Enter the out-of-band management address range as shown below:

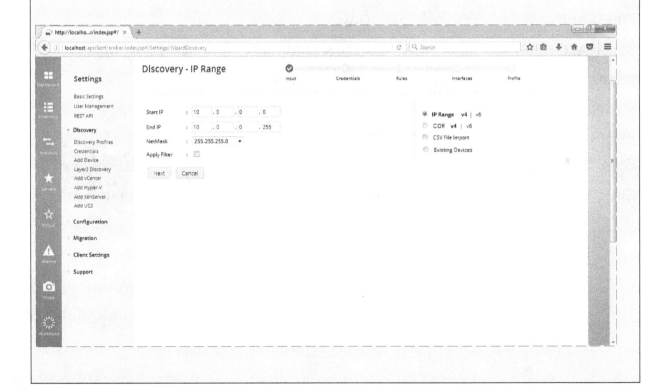

By clicking on "Next", a web page will be prompted for user credentials we defined on R1 and Firewall. Enter the credentials of SNMPv3 AuthNoPriv model. Select MD5 as hashing algorithm as it has to match with R1's configuration.

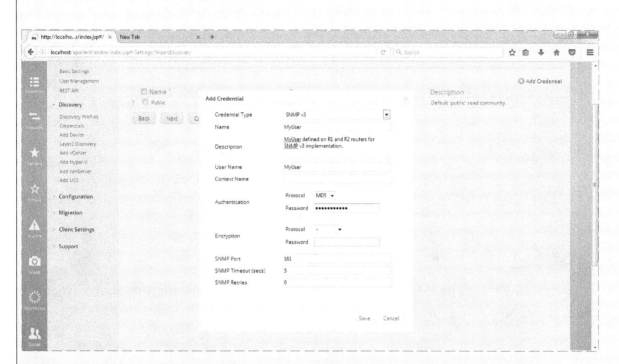

After clicking on finish, OPManager will responding to incoming SNMP traffic.

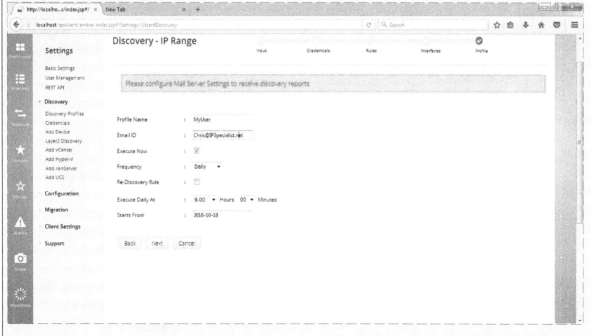

Same procedure must also be performed for Firewall network (1.1.1.0/30).

After completing the steps for firewall network, OPManager must identify router R1 and Firewall after completing discovery process as shown below:

By double clicking on R1 and Firewall, it is clear that OP Manager has identified device category and its model number along with interfaces and other features.

After adding every device from discovery process, Dashboard can be used to view important information. Importance of securing such crucial information displayed by SNMP should be clear at this stage.

SNMP MindMap

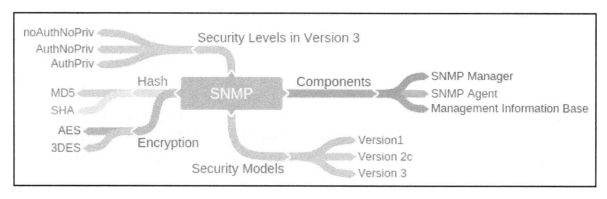

Figure 20- SNMP MindMap

Chapter 3: Management Services on Cisco Devices

Technology Brief

While previous chapters focused on different security attacks and mitigation against them by configuring different features of Cisco devices, this chapter focuses on different management services that keep network engineers up to date regarding changing in network design.

In reality, these services also pose security threat in bigger perspective as hacker can also sniff traffic of management services and can create greater problems. One of the main objective of this chapter is to configure the more secure version of these management services like *SNMP v3, NetFlow,* etc.

NetFlow

While SNMP and Syslog helps network administrators for management and troubleshooting of network infrastructure, Netflow provides the deep insight of what's happening inside a network. There are certain cases where different services may be facing downtime or delay issues, for example, IP telephony being affected if some users are using bandwidth-hungry applications. In such cases, enabling Netflow on layer3 device helps in identifying the users or devices, which are consuming most of the bandwidth in different perspectives. For example, by analyzing the percentage of traffic generated for different protocols like ICMP, HTTP, TELNET, etc. Similarly, NetFlow information regarding the top destination hits, top talkers on network segment can also help in tuning the overall bandwidth management of network.

One of the major advantages of using NetFlow instead of protocol analyzer is that Netflow works just like our phone bills that contains the history and call duration of different phone numbers over the period and no conversation is included in it. Unlike protocol analyzers, which require the mirroring of every single packet going either in or out of interface, NetFlow keeps the cache for short amount of time although a limit can also be set on it via Sampler option.

Three basic components of Netflow to be able to work on a network are:

Component	Description
Monitor	Monitor collects the information while traffic flows either inbound or outbound direction of router interface and cache information for period of time
Exporter	Exporter then collects the cached data and ships it to the management station for analyzing
Collector	Management station would be running some Netflow collector software, which shows the network statistics in a user-friendly way by using tabular or graphical methods

Table 17- NetFlow Components and their Descriptions

Just like enterprise network engineers can use Netflow for internal network tuning, Service Providers can also use Netflow for following purposes:

- Check and balance of bandwidth; analyzing the usage of network services by different clients
- Charging the clients as per resource utilization
- Using NetFlow statistics for routine network tuning and managed services

NetFlows Mindmap

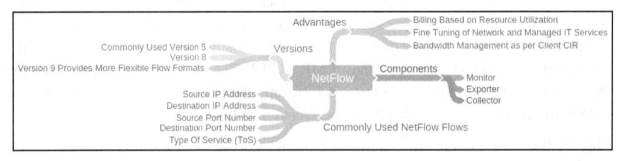

Figure 21- NetFlow's MindMap

Network Time Protocol (NTP)

One of the most important feature of Logging is timestamp of an event. An attacker may want to change the time settings so that user may be unaware of an event. In order to synchronize the time over, the *Network Time Protocol (NTP)* is used. NTPv3 being latest is used due to its support for encryption. There is also a newer version of NTP, i.e., NTPv4, which is considered an extension to NTPv3 and it supports both IPV4 and IPV6 along with some enhanced security.

NTP uses UDP port number 123. Although Cisco devices can be set as NTP Clients of publically available NTP servers, we can set a single device in network infrastructure as NTP server and all devices synchronize their time to that device. One of the advantages of using NTP service is to correlate different events. If time is tampered, it would be impossible to find the root cause of the main problem.

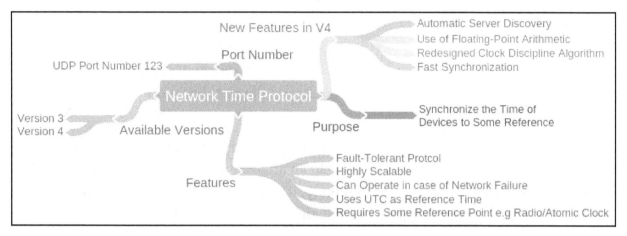

Figure 22- NTP Mind Map

Secure Copy Protocol (SCP)

SCP stands for Secure Copy Protocol used for transferring files between client and server machines. SCP uses SSH for data transfer and authentication hence adds both authenticity and confidentiality to the whole process. SCP allows users with appropriate authorization level to securely copy any file from that exists in the Cisco IOS File System. A third party software is also used on workstation to copy files. Similarly, to copy file from one Cisco device to another, we can use *copy* command.

Secure File Transfer Protocol (SFTP)

Secure File Transfer Protocol (SFTP) is preferred over FTP whose operation is performed completely in plain text. Just like SCP, SFTP uses SSH in its underlying process to securely transfer data between local and remote peers.

Unlike SCP, SFTP has a lot of other capabilities besides secure file transfer. For example, letting SFTP clients resume interrupted file transfers, removing specific files and directory listings.

CDP and its Security Implications

Cisco Discovery Protocol (CDP), as name depicts, is a Cisco proprietary protocol, which is majorly used to identify the different parameters of attached networking devices. CDP is

also used in On-Demand Routing (ODR) where routing information is sent within CDP packets. Depending on IOS version and platform, CDP advertises the following type-length-value fields in its message:

- Device ID
- Address
- Port ID
- Capabilities
- Version
- Platform
- Native VLAN

- Full/Half Duplex
- MTU
- SysName
- SysObjectID
- Management Address
- Physical Location
- VTP

CDP should be disabled to prevent an attacker getting the overall view of networking topology. CDP works at layer 2 and may help an attacker to redesign the attack according to the physical topology of network. Similarly, if Link Layer Discovery Protocol (LLDP) is used which is IEEE implementation of CDP, then it must be disabled as well.

DNSSEC and its Importance

Everything on public internet has some unique IP address assigned to it. Thanks to the Domain Name System (DNS), end-users are not required to remember the unique IP addresses. Instead, a fully qualified domain name (uniquely assigned to different entities) can be used by end-users and DNS will automatically convert it to the desired IP address. As far as Layer 4 information is concerned, DNS can use both TCP and UDP port number 53.

DNS is composed of a hierarchical domain namespace that contains a tree-like data structure of linked domain names (nodes). Domain name space uses Resource Records (RRs) that store information about the domain. The tree-like data structure for the domain name space starts at the root zone "." that is the top-most level of the DNS hierarchy. Although it is not typically displayed in user applications, the DNS root is represented as a trailing dot in a Fully Qualified Domain Name (FQDN). For example, the right-most dot in "www.Cisco.com." represents the root zone. From the root zone, the DNS hierarchy (tree) is then split into sub-domain zones (branches).

Each domain name is composed of one or more labels. Labels are separated with a "." character and may contain a maximum of 63 characters. A FQDN may contain a maximum of 255 characters, including the "." character. Labels are constructed from right to left, where the label at the far right is the Top-Level Domain (TLD) for the domain name. The following example shows how to identify the TLD for a domain name:

"com" is the TLD for 'www.Cisco.com' because it is the label that is farthest to the right.

Consider an example where a DNS query hits the server.

- If the information in requested query exists in the server (authoritative or cached), then server will reply with the requested information.

If server does not have the requested information, then one of the following actions may take place:

- If the server is configured with DNS recursion, then it will query other DNS servers, and after updating its cache with new information, it will reply to the DNS client
- If the server is not configured with DNS recursion and RD flag is not set in incoming query, the DNS server can provide information regarding other DNS servers, which might have information requested in original query
- If requested data does not exist, then DNS server might respond back with "no such data exists" message
- If DNS server is misconfigured, then it may send error code as response to DNS query

DNSSEC

By incorporating cryptographic signatures in the DNS information, the DNS client can make sure the information that is requested from DNS server is correct and is not altered except from the authoritative DNS source. Although DNSSEC works exactly like DNS, however, there are some differences as well. One of the most important difference is that DNSSEC packets may exceed 512 bytes, which may be dropped by conventional policies used by ASA and PIX firewalls.

Case Study

In this section case study from last chapter will be used as this chapter introduced some new methodologies of networking device hardening by GUI tools.

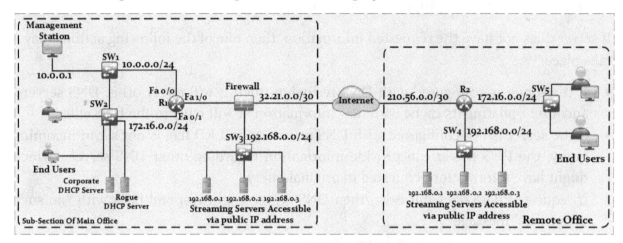

Figure 23- Management Services on Cisco Devices Case Study

Lab 3.1: Configuration of NetFlow Exporter on Cisco Routers, Switches and ASA

As explained in previous section of NetFlow, one of the components of NetFlow, i.e., exporter needs to be configured on a device, whose interface traffic needs to be analyzed. Exporter will send this traffic back to the management station where dedicated NetFlow Analyzer software is running. Commercially available NetFlow software have their own requirements. For example, the software used in this lab discovers the NetFlow devices via SNMP. So previously, configure SNMP lab must be implemented before starting this lab.

NetFlow exporter will be configured on R1 and Firewall in this lab, and then different types of traffic will be generated from management station to analyze the behavior of NetFlow.

R1
R1(config)# snmp-server view MyView iso included

R1#sho snmp engineID

`Local SNMP engineID: 800000090300C2061B750000`

R1(config)#snmp-server engineID remote 10.0.0.1 800000090300C2061B750000

R1(config)#snmp-server group MyGroup v3 auth read MyView access SNMP-ACL

R1(config)#IP access-list standard SNMP-ACL

R1(config-std-nacl)#permit host 10.0.0.1

R1(config)# snmp-server user MyUser MyGroup v3 auth md5 P@$$word:10

Above commands configure SNMPv3 on Route R1 with read access to management station (10.0.0.1) only.

R1(config)# flow exporter EXPORT-1

R1(config-flow-exporter)# destination 10.0.0.1

R1(config-flow-exporter)#transport udp 9996

R1(config-flow-exporter)#source FastEthernet 0/0

Above commands create an exporter object with name EXPORT-1. UDP port number 9996 is configured for NetFlow. As of our lab scenario, all traffic from management station hits fastEthernet 0/0 of R1. So FastEthernet 0/0 is configured as source interface for capturing NetFlow statistics.

R1(config)#flow monitor MONITOR-1

R1(config-flow-monitor)#record NetFlow ipv4 original input

R1(config-flow-monitor)#exporter EXPORT-1

Above commands define the record type, i.e., the type of data collected by NetFlow instance. This information will be exported to management station for NetFlow Analyzer by EXPORT-1. In the final step, go to the desired interface and apply the monitor instance in desired direction.

R1(config)#interface FastEthernet 0/0

R1(config-if)#IP flow monitor MONITOR-1 input

Verification

Open SolarWinds real-time NetFlow Analyzer from start menu of management-station. The following screen would appear:

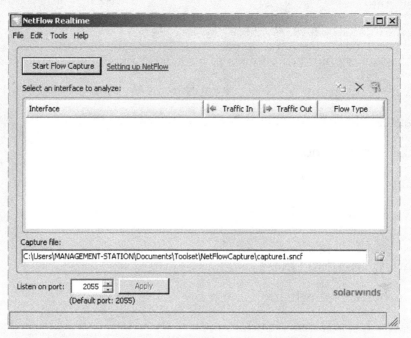

Click button to define the SNMPv3 credentials for R1.

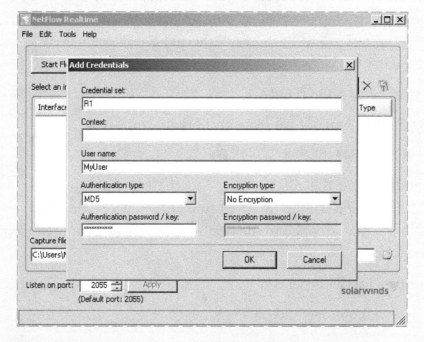

After defining the SNMPv3 credentials, click "Test" button for verification.

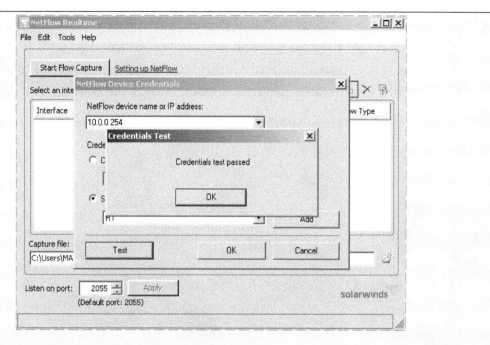

After clicking "OK", R1 should appear in main window of NetFlow Analyzer. Change the port to 9996, select the FastEtherneto/0 interface of R1 and click **Start Flow Capture** to show NetFlow statistics. In order to observe some meaningful results, make multiple SSH/TELNET sessions to R1 and multiple PING sessions with multiple devices from management and END-USER LAN.

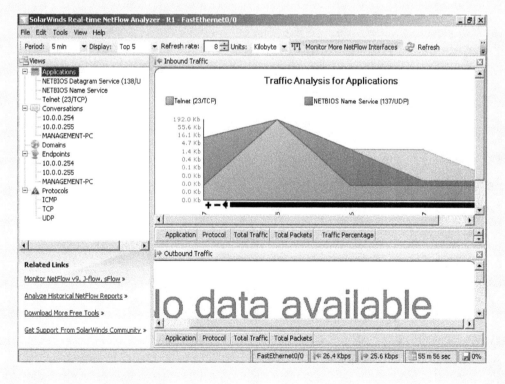

In case of production environment, where different protocols based traffic gets generated every minute; the above graph will show multiple session information in that case. As in our lab scenario, there are limited devices involved and only PING, TELNET/SSH traffic is generated protocol section is showing only ICMP, TCP and UDP.

To check the configuration of exporter instance in router, use the following command:

R1#show flow exporter EXPORT-1

```
Flow Exporter EXPORT-1:
   Description:                  User defined
   Tranport Configuration:
     Destination IP address:     10.0.0.1
     Source IP address:          10.0.0.254
     Source Interface:           FastEthernet0/0
     Transport Protocol:         UDP
     Destination Port:           9996
     Source Port:                56971
     DSCP:                       0x0
     TTL:                        255
```

Similarly, to check the configuration of monitor instance in router, use the following command:

R1#show flow monitor MONITOR-1

```
Flow Monitor MONITOR-1:
   Description:          User defined
   Flow Record:          netflow ipv4 original-input
   Flow Exporter:        EXPORT-1
   Cache:
     Type:               normal
     Status:             allocated
     Size:               4096 entries / 311316 bytes
     Inactive Timeout:   15 secs
     Active Timeout:     1800 secs
     Update Timeout:     1800 secs
```

To check the cached data stored by monitor instance on router, use the following command. Depending on number of connections passing the specific interface, the size of output may vary.

R1# show flow monitor name MONITOR-1 cache

Cache type:	Normal
Cache size:	4096
Current entries:	4
High Watermark:	7
Flows added:	26
Flows aged:	22
- Active timeout (1800 secs)	0
- Inactive timeout (15 secs)	22
- Event aged	0
- Watermark aged	0
- Emergency aged	0
IP TOS:	0x00
IP PROTOCOL:	1
IPV4 SOURCE ADDRESS:	10.0.0.1
IPV4 DESTINATION ADDRESS:	172.16.0.1
TRNS SOURCE PORT:	0
TRNS DESTINATION PORT:	2048
INTERFACE INPUT:	Fa0/0
FLOW SAMPLER ID:	0
interface output:	Fa0/1
ipv4 next hop address:	172.16.0.1
tcp flags:	0x00

IP source as:	0
IP destination as:	0
ipv4 source mask:	/24
ipv4 destination mask:	/24
timestamp first:	4711456

```
timestamp last:                              6203320
counter packets:                             2786
counter bytes:                               2864008
```

As NetFlow configuration on device running in production environment may result in high processing, it's a good idea to limit the NetFlow traffic by using sampling feature.

R1 (config)# sampler SAMPLER-1

R1 (config)# mode deterministic 1 out-of 10

R1(Config) # interface FastEthernet 0/0

R1(config-if)# IP flow monitor MONITOR-1 sampler SAMPLER-1 input

As shown in above figure, deterministic mode of sampling is used in which 1 out of every 10 packets will be cached. Similarly, on interface level sub-command, sampler keyword must be added to actually apply the sampling feature of NetFlow. The following command can be used to verify the sampler configuration in IOS:

R1# show sampler SAMPLER-1

```
Sampler SAMPLER-1:
   ID:            0
   Description:   User defined
   Type:          deterministic
   Rate:          1 out of 10
   Samples:       0
   Requests:      0
   Users (0):
```

ASA

SNMP needs to be configured first before moving to NetFlow configuration.

FIREWALL(config)# snmp-server enable

FIREWALL(config)# snmp-server enable traps all

FIREWALL(config)# snmp-server group MyGroup v3 auth

FIREWALL(config)# snmp-server user MyUser MyGroup v3 auth md5 P@$$word:10

FIREWALL(config)# snmp-server host inside 10.0.0.1 version 3 MyUser

Above commands configure SNMPv3 on ASA FIREWALL with read access to management station (10.0.0.1) only.

FIREWALL(config)# flow-export destination inside 10.0.0.1 9996

FIREWALL(config)# access-list flow_export_acl permit IP any any

FIREWALL(config)# class-map flow_export_class

FIREWALL(config-cmap)# match access-list flow_export_acl

FIREWALL(config-cmap)# exit

FIREWALL(config)# policy-map global_policy

FIREWALL(config-pmap)# class flow_export_class

FIREWALL(config-pmap-c)# flow-export event-type all destination 10.0.0.1

Above commands re-edit the global policy being applied on ASA with another class map flow_export_class and sends the NetFlow information to destination 10.0.0.1

Verification

Add the ASA in Netflow Analyzer just like R1.

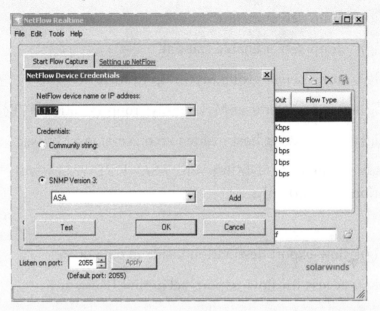

After entering correct SNMP credentials as defined above, FIREWALL must be shown in main dashboard of NetFlow analyzer software.

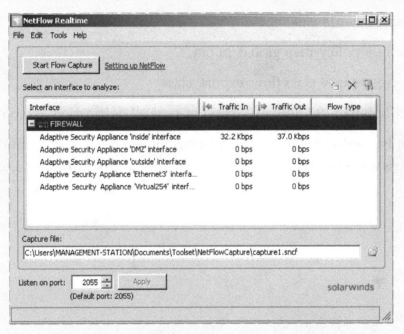

To verify the flow export output on ASA use the following commands:

FIREWALL# show flow-export counters

```
destination: inside 10.0.0.1 9996
```

```
Statistics:

   packets sent                        199

Errors:

   block allocation failure            0

   invalid interface                   0

   template send failure               0

   no route to collector               0

   failed to get lock on block         0

   source port allocation failure      0


FIREWALL# show access-list flow_export_acl

access-list flow_export_acl; 1 elements; name hash: 0xe30f1adf

access-list flow_export_acl line 1 extended permit IP any (hitcnt=771) 0x759f5ecf
```

Lab 3.2: Configuration of NTP and Syslog Based Logging on Cisco Routers, Switches and ASA

In this lab, primary focus is correction of timestamps of system logs and events by using NTP. Normally the perimeter edge router gets time from public NTP servers available on internet. Then this edge router acts as NTP server for internal LAN devices. NTP server is also available as standalone device, which uses radio or atomic clock in its operation. NTP helps in correlating events by the time system logs are received by Syslog servers. NTP uses UDP port number 123, and its whole communication is based on coordinated universal time (UTC).

NTP uses a term known as *stratum* to describe the distance between NTP server and device. It is just like TTL number that decreases every hop a packet passes by. Starting from one, stratum number increases by every hop. For example, if we see stratum number 10 on local router, it means that NTP server is nine hops away. Securing NTP is also an important aspect as attacker may change time at first place to mislead the forensic teams who investigate and correlate the events to find the root cause of attack.

In this part, router R1 will act as NTP server. Switches and ASA will act as NTP client to R1. NTPV3 also supports authentication, which will be used in this lab.

R1

First set the local clock of router depending your geographical region.

Use show clock command to see current time.

R1#show clock

```
*00:01:38.203 UTC Fri Mar 1 2002
```

R1#clock set 00:00:00 17 FEB 2017

```
Feb 17 00:00:00.003: %SYS-6-CLOCKUPDATE: System clock has been updated from 00:
02:22 UTC Fri Mar 1 2002 to 00:00:00 UTC Fri Feb 17 2017, configured from console by
console.
```

R2#show clock

```
00:01:16.931 UTC Fri Feb 17 2017
```

It is clear from above command that clock set command has indeed changed the time. Now configure R1 as NTP server with following configuration:

R1(config)#NTP master 10

R1(config)#NTP authentication-key 1 md5 P@$$word:10

NTP master command configure router R1 as NTP server with 10 as stratum number it will

advertise. In the second command MD5, based authentication key is defined. Now access switch SW1 to configure as NTP client.

SW1

First, check the current date of R1 using show clock command.

SW1#show clock

```
*06:14:45.270 UTC Wed Jan 18 2017
```

SW1(config)#NTP authenticate

SW1 (config)#NTP authentication-key 1 md5 P@$$word:10

SW1 (config)#NTP trusted-key 1

SW1(config)#NTP server 10.0.0.254 key 1

In above commands, NTP server IP address along with md5 based authentication key is

defined. NTP trusted-key command specifies which key should be used for authenticating time source.

Verification

Show NTP status command can be used to verify connection with NTP Server.

SW1#show NTP status

```
Clock is unsynchronized, stratum 16, no reference clock

nominal freq is 250.0000 Hz, actual freq is 250.0000 Hz, precision is 2**10

NTP uptime is 9600 (1/100 of seconds), resolution is 4000

reference time is 00000000.00000000 (00:00:00.000 UTC Mon Jan 1 1900)

clock offset is 0.0000 msec, root delay is 0.00 msec

root dispersion is 1.44 msec, peer dispersion is 0.00 msec

loop filter state is 'NSET' (Never set), drift is 0.000000000 s/s

system poll interval is 64, never updated.
```

NTP client takes a little more time than other protocols to synchronize with NTP server (maybe 5 minutes or more). It is advised to manually set the clock of NTP client as close to NTP server's time as possible to minimize the sync time between client and server. Show NTP association command can be used to check the IP address and other information related to NTP server.

SW1#show NTP associations

Address	ref clock	st	when	poll	reach	delay	offset	disp
~10.0.0.254	127.127.7.1	10	37	64	1	6.842	26609.6	3938.4

```
 * sys.peer, # selected, + candidate, - outlier, x false ticker, ~ configured
```

Above output shows that 10.0.0.254 is configured as NTP server. After some time check again with above commands, it must show synced clock with NTP server.

Issuing same command on NTP Server shows the following output:

R1#show NTP associations

Address	ref clock	st	when	poll	reach	delay	offset	disp
*~127.127.7.1	127.127.7.1	9	46	64	377	0.0	0.00	0.0

```
 * master (synced), # master (unsynced), + selected, - candidate, ~ configured
! 127.127.7.1 means that R1 itself is NTP server.
```

```
SW1#show NTP status

Clock is synchronized, stratum 11, reference is 10.0.0.254
nominal freq is 250.0000 Hz, actual freq is 250.0001 Hz, precision is 2**18
reference time is DC50BC0B.A0F010B7 (00:02:19.628 UTC Fri Feb 17 2017)
clock offset is -26.5792 msec, root delay is 11.87 msec
root dispersion is 42.53 msec, peer dispersion is 15.91 msec
```

```
SW1#sho NTP associations

Address            ref clock     st    when   poll   reach  delay  offset      disp
*~10.0.0.254       127.127.7.1   10    53     64     377    11.9   -26.58      15.9
 * master (synced), # master (unsynced), + selected, - candidate, ~ configured
```

Firewall
In order to configure ASA firewall as NTP client to R1, use the following commands:

FIREWALL(config)#NTP authentication-key 1 md5 P@$$word:10

FIREWALL(config)#NTP authenticate

FIREWALL(config)#NTP server 1.1.1.1 key 1

FIREWALL(config)#NTP trusted-key 1

In the last section of this lab, Syslog logging will be enabled on router R1 and ASA FIREWALL to send every message being generated to the management station where dedicated Syslog Server is running.

R1
Logging command is used to specify the IP address of Syslog server.

R1(config)# logging 10.0.0.1

R1(config)# logging trap debugging

R1(config)#service timestamps debug datetime msec

R1(config)#service timestamps log datetime msec

> Logging trap command tells router to send every log/event up to debugging level of Syslog. Service timestamps command is used to include timestamp in log messages.

Firewall

FIREWALL(config)# logging enable

FIREWALL(config)# logging host inside 10.0.0.1

FIREWALL(config)# logging trap debugging

FIREWALL(config)# logging timestamp

Verification

In order to verify logging settings on ASA, use the following command:

FIREWALL# sho logging setting

```
Syslog logging: disabled
    Facility: 20
    Timestamp logging: enabled
    Standby logging: disabled
    Debug-trace logging: disabled
    Console logging: disabled
    Monitor logging: disabled
    Buffer logging: disabled
    Trap logging: level debugging, facility 20, 0 messages logged
        Logging to inside 10.0.0.1
    Permit-host down logging: disabled
    History logging: disabled
    Device ID: disabled
    Mail logging: disabled
    ASDM logging: disabled
```

Similarly, on IOS, use the following command:

R₁#show logging

```
Syslog logging: enabled (12 messages dropped, 0 messages rate-limited,
                0 flushes, 0 overruns, xml disabled, filtering disabled)


No Active Message Discriminator.
No Inactive Message Discriminator.


    Console logging: level debugging, 2436 messages logged, xml disabled,
                filtering disabled
    Monitor logging: level debugging, 0 messages logged, xml disabled,
                filtering disabled
    Buffer logging:  disabled, xml disabled,
                filtering disabled
    Logging Exception size (4096 bytes)
    Count and timestamp logging messages: disabled
    Persistent logging: disabled


No active filter modules.


ESM: 0 messages dropped


    Trap logging: level debugging, 190 message lines logged
        Logging to 10.0.0.1 (udp port 514, audit disabled,
            authentication disabled, encryption disabled, link up),
            3 message lines logged,
            0 message lines rate-limited,
            0 message lines dropped-by-MD,
            xml disabled, sequence number disabled
            filtering disabled
```

Open source *3CDaemon* server used in this lab contains Syslog server along with FTP and other servers. Click on the 3CD icon on start menu to start it and view its operations. As

OP Manager is also installed on same management station. We may need to stop manage engine service before starting Syslog server.

To stop manage engine service, type "services.msc" in start menu and stop the Manage Engine OPManager service.

Following figure shows few logs received by Syslog server:

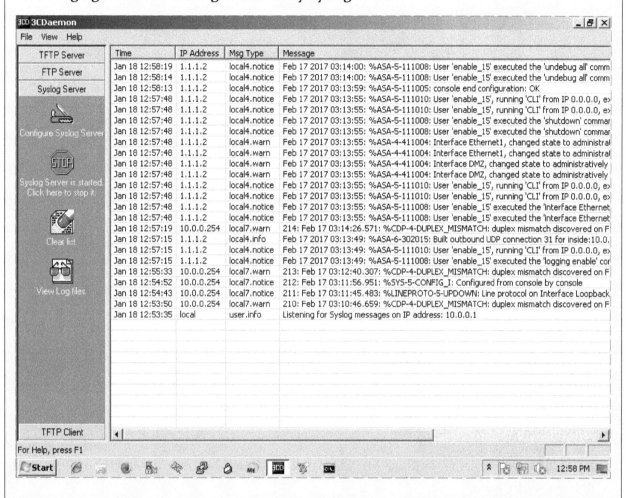

By shutting interface or creating a loopback interface will generate the Syslog messages and it will appear on Syslog server dashboard.

Lab 3.3: Disabling CDP on Cisco Routers and Switches

R1

R1#show CDP neighbours

```
Capability Codes: R - Router, T - Trans Bridge, B - Source Route Bridge
                  S - Switch, H - Host, I - IGMP, r - Repeater


Device ID    Local Intrfce     Holdtme      Capability   Platform     Port ID
SW1          Fas 0/0           153          R S I        Linux Uni    Eth 0/0
SW2          Fas 0/1           164          R S I        Linux Uni    Eth 0/0
```

As CPD is enabled by default, the above command shows a lot of meaningful information. This information can be used by attacker in order to get the overall or segment of network topology.

To disable it globally, use the following command:

R1(config)#no cdp run

R1#show cdp neighbours

`% CDP is not enabled`

Above command will disable the CDP on every interface of device. In order to disable CDP on specific interface, go to the interface configuration mode and use the following command:

R1(config-if)# no cdp enable

Same configuration also applies on Cisco switches as command-set on routers and switches are the same.

Lab 3.4: Troubleshooting/Analyzing Cisco ASA by using Packet-Tracer and Packet-Capture and Botnet Filtering Features via CLI/ASDM

Cisco ASA has built-in features of packet capture and packet tracer, which can be used for troubleshooting purposes. In this lab, CLI section will be covered followed by performing the same task via ASDM.

ASA

As of current policy, no traffic is allowed from outside to inside/Dmz interface. As traffic from high to low-security level is permitted by default, this can be analyzed by using packet-tracer command.

ciscoasa(config)# packet-tracer input inside tcp 10.0.0.1 echo 192.168.0.2 echo

```
Phase: 1

Type: ACCESS-LIST

Subtype:

Result: ALLOW

Config:

Implicit Rule

Additional Information:

MAC Access list

Phase: 2

Type: ROUTE-LOOKUP

Subtype: input

Result: ALLOW

Config:

Additional Information:

in   192.168.0.0    255.255.255.0   DMZ

Phase: 3

Type: ACCESS-LIST

Subtype: log

Result: ALLOW

Config:

access-group 100 in interface inside

access-list 100 extended permit ip 10.0.0.0 255.255.255.0 any

Additional Information:
```

```
Phase: 4

Type: IP-OPTIONS

Subtype:

Result: ALLOW

Config:

Additional Information:

Phase: 5

Type: IP-OPTIONS

Subtype:

Result: ALLOW

Config:

Additional Information:

Phase: 6

Type: FLOW-CREATION

Subtype:

Result: ALLOW

Config:

Additional Information:

New flow created with id 16, packet dispatched to next module

Result:

input-interface: inside

input-status: up

input-line-status: up

output-interface: DMZ

output-status: up

output-line-status: up

Action: allow
```

As default route is used on ASA FIREWALL and traffic from inside to outside interface is allowed by default, each phase of packet tracer results in ALLOW. Let us use packet-tracer to see whether traffic from outside to inside is allowed or not.

```
ciscoasa(config)# packet-tracer input DMZ tcp 10.0.0.1 echo 192.168.0.2 echo

Phase: 1

Type: ACCESS-LIST
```

```
Subtype:

Result: ALLOW

Config:

Implicit Rule

Additional Information:

MAC Access list

Phase: 2

Type: ROUTE-LOOKUP

Subtype: input

Result: ALLOW

Config:

Additional Information:

in   192.168.0.0     255.255.255.0    DMZ

Phase: 3

Type: ACCESS-LIST

Subtype:

Result: DROP

Config:

Implicit Rule

Additional Information:
```

```
Result:

input-interface: DMZ

input-status: up

input-line-status: up

output-interface: DMZ

output-status: up

output-line-status: up

Action: drop

Drop-reason: (acl-drop) Flow is denied by configured rule
```

Last line clearly states the reason for dropping the traffic. In order to allow such sessions from outside to inside, Access-list needs to be applied on outside interface permitting the desired traffic.

Another cool feature that comes preloaded in ASA firewall is packet capturing capability. In order to implement Packet capture from CLI, the steps below need to followed:

1) Create an ACL from traffic that need to be captured.

2) Then, start the capture on desired interface.

3) Then, display or save the packet capture.

4) Stop the packet capture and clear the buffer as it takes significant space in RAM.

Default buffer size is 512 KB, which can be increased as per scenario. It should be kept in mind that buffer for packet capture is not FIFO in nature. Once it is filled, then it would not be overwritten by new data.

FIREWALL(config)# access-list packetcapACL permit IP any any

FIREWALL(config)# capture captureinside access-list packetcapACL interface inside

Now, start continuous ping from management-station to R2 (210.56.0.2) and use the following command to see the packet capture.

```
FIREWALL# show capture captureinside


33 packets captured


1: 06:26:10.673213 10.0.0.1 > 169.254.114.114: icmp: echo request

2: 06:26:10.906386 10.0.0.1 > 169.254.114.114: icmp: echo request

3: 06:26:11.144935 10.0.0.1 > 169.254.114.114: icmp: echo request

4: 06:26:11.398783 10.0.0.1 > 169.254.114.114: icmp: echo request

5: 06:26:13.919508 10.0.0.1 > 169.254.114.114: icmp: echo request

6: 06:26:14.156196 10.0.0.1 > 169.254.114.114: icmp: echo request

7: 06:26:14.387598 10.0.0.1 > 169.254.114.114: icmp: echo request
```

Although most the ICMP messages have been clipped in above output, the total number of packets captured will be displayed at the top of show capture command's output.

To stop the packet capture, use the following command:

FIREWALL(config)# no capture captureinside

FIREWALL(config)# show capture captureinside

`ERROR: Capture <captureinside> does not exist`

FIREWALL(config)# show capture

In the last section of this lab, same tasks will be performed via ASDM. In order to allow access ASA via GUI, HTTPS access for specific IP needs to be allowed first. The following commands create a privilege level 15 username and allow HTTPS access for management station (10.0.0.1) from inside interface.

FIREWALL(config)# username IPSpecialist password P@$$word:10 privilege 15

FIREWALL(config)# http server enable

FIREWALL(config)# http 10.0.0.1 255.255.255.255 inside

FIREWALL(config)# aaa authentication http console LOCAL

FIREWALL(config)# ssl encryption 3des-sha1 aes128-sha1 aes256-sha1

Open ASDM by clicking pinned to taskbar. The following screen would appear. Use the above-defined credentials to log in.

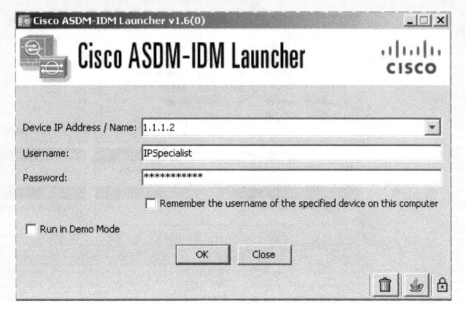

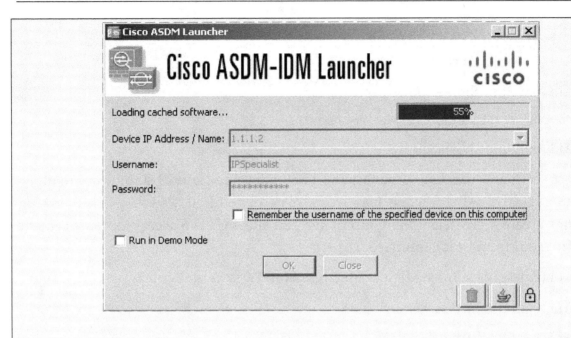

After loading, the following dashboard will appear.

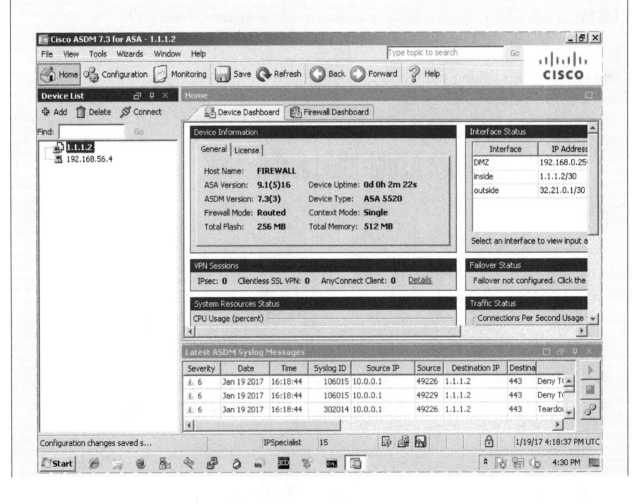

As discussed in Chapter 2, ASDM is one-to-one management software, i.e., only one firewall can be configured at a time. As shown in the above figure, the leftmost table shows the list of firewalls being added in ASDM.

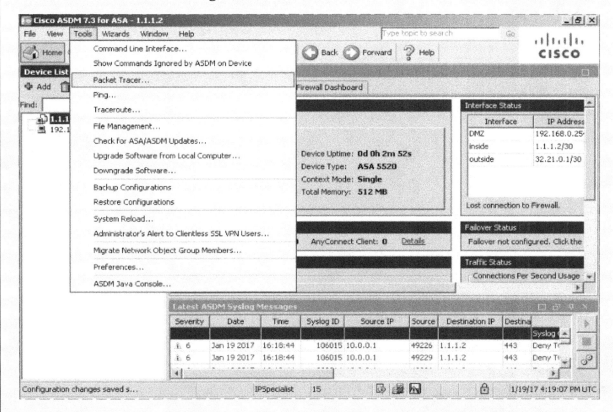

As shown in above figure, click Tools -> Packet Tracer to use this utility as used earlier in CLI mode.

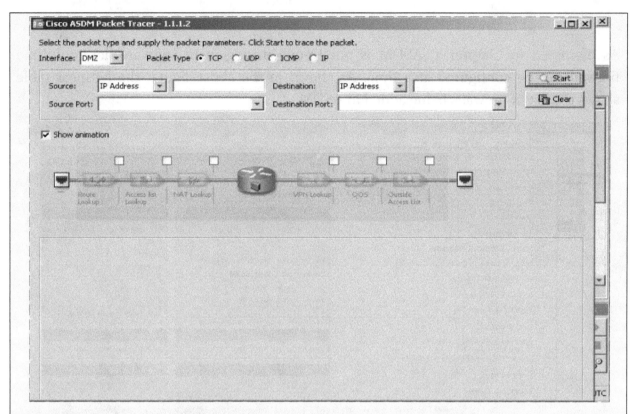

Select the source interface, provide layer 3 and layer 4 information of desired packet and click [Q Start] button to see if desired packet with provided information can pass firewall or not.

Below figures shows the same tests performed in CLI section.

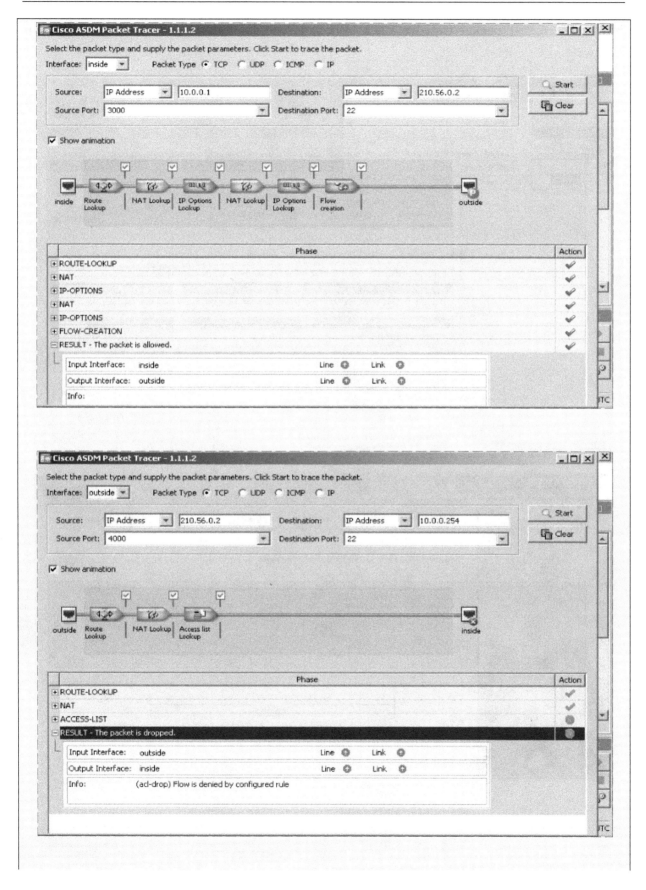

Similarly, to test packet capture, click "Wizards" -> "Packet Capture Wizard" as shown below.

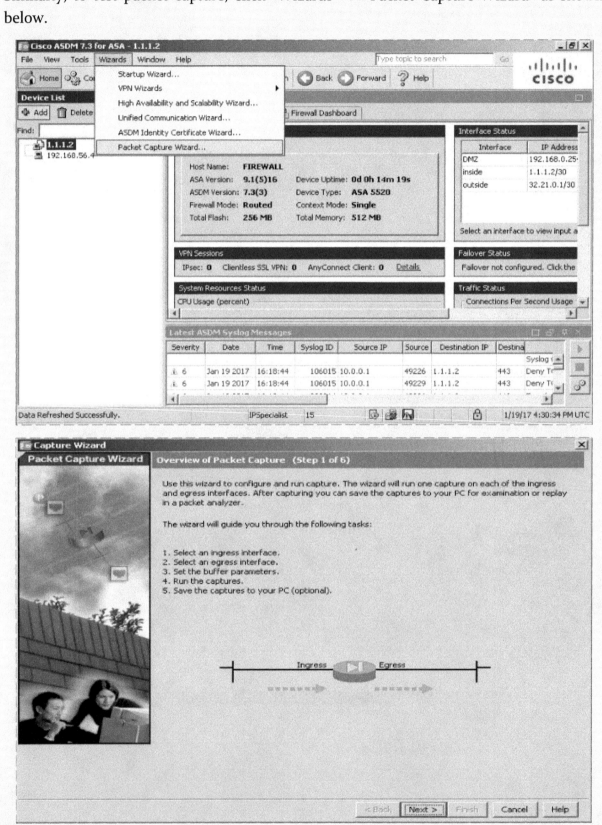

Click "Next".

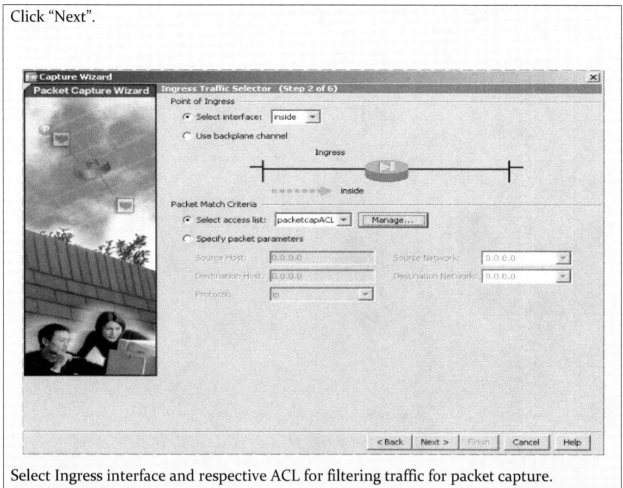

Select Ingress interface and respective ACL for filtering traffic for packet capture.

Click "Next".

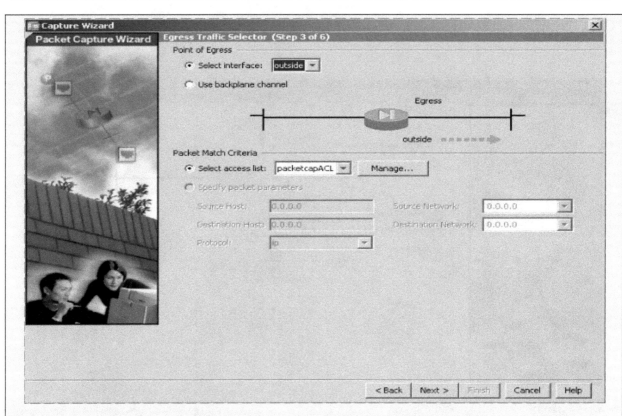

Select Egress interface and respective ACL for filtering traffic for packet capture.

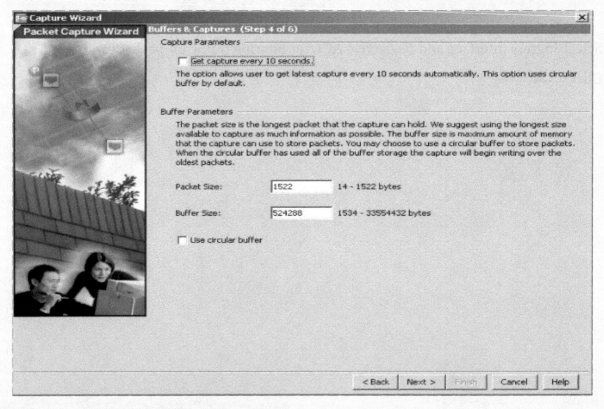

Set the optional buffer size and click "Next".

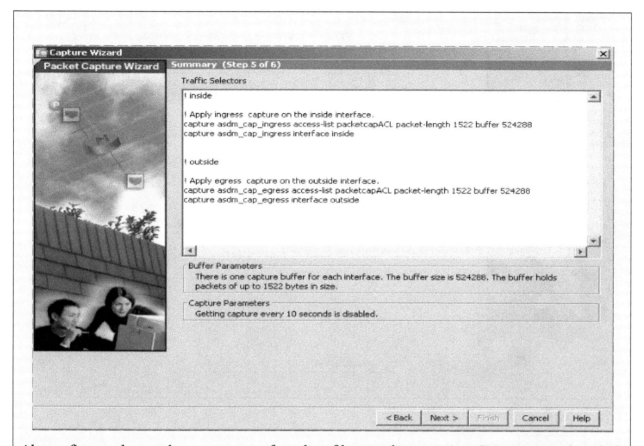

Above figure shows the summary of packet filter and respective CLI commands. Click "Next".

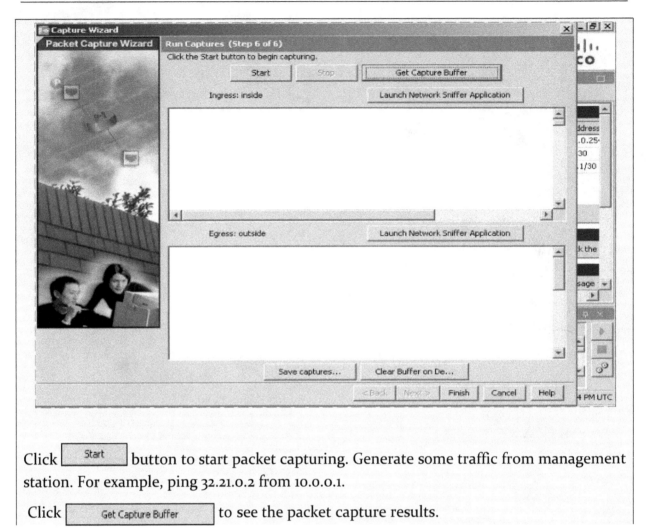

Click [Start] button to start packet capturing. Generate some traffic from management station. For example, ping 32.21.0.2 from 10.0.0.1.

Click [Get Capture Buffer] to see the packet capture results.

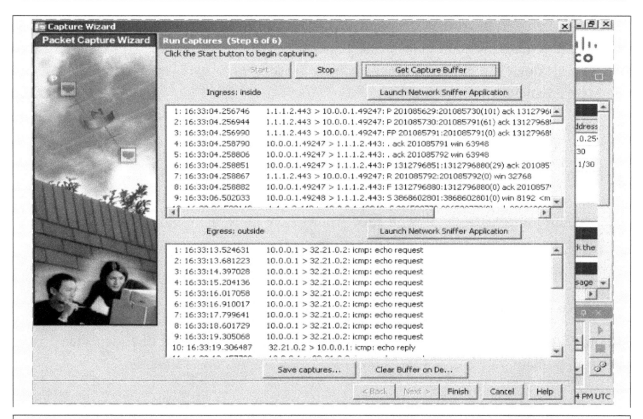

Packet capture can also be save in known file formats, for example, PCAP format based file for Wire-Shark by clicking | Save captures... | button and then specifying the file format.

Botnet Filtering

Malware is an umbrella term used to refer to a variety of forms of hostile or intrusive software, including computer viruses, worms, Trojan horses, ransomware, spyware, adware, scareware, and other malicious programs. It can take the form of executable code, scripts, active content, and other software.

Identifying malware as it attempts to enter the network or already residing in network infrastructure is one of the most tedious job of a security-concerned person. There are several factors, which make its identification a little bit difficult. Any new malware created is undetectable from signature-based detection tools. Normally, malwareis embedded in trusted applications and sent over the protocols that are traditionally permitted in firewalls and Access Lists of network devices like HTTP and HTTPS traffic. A dedicated human resource would be required if every single piece of data, which traverse across the network needs to be monitored. Increased usage of encryption also adds another layer of complexity for an organization to classify malicious traffic.

Botnet filtering feature of Cisco ASA helps in identifying and filtering the network connections made by such malware installed in a group of hundreds and thousands of machines known as botnet. Botnet filtering feature uses two types of databases for detecting malicious activities namely:

- Dynamic Database
- Static Database

Dynamic database includes signatures and information of IPs and domain names, which are known for some malicious encounter in the past. Dynamic database always gets updated and automatically downloaded from Cisco. Dynamic database is managed and updated by Security Intelligent Operation of Cisco. Apart from dynamic database, network administrators can also input their own database of manual IP addresses and domain names for filtering (Blacklists). Similarly, by using whitelists, user can bypass certain IP addresses and domain names from botnet filtering.

In order to perform above functions, Cisco ASA needs to be a DNS Client so that it can perform domain to IP conversion as provided by dynamic/static databases.

Firewall

After accessing Firewall via ASDM, click [Configuration] -> [Firewall]

[Botnet Traffic Filter] to configure different settings of botnet filtering.

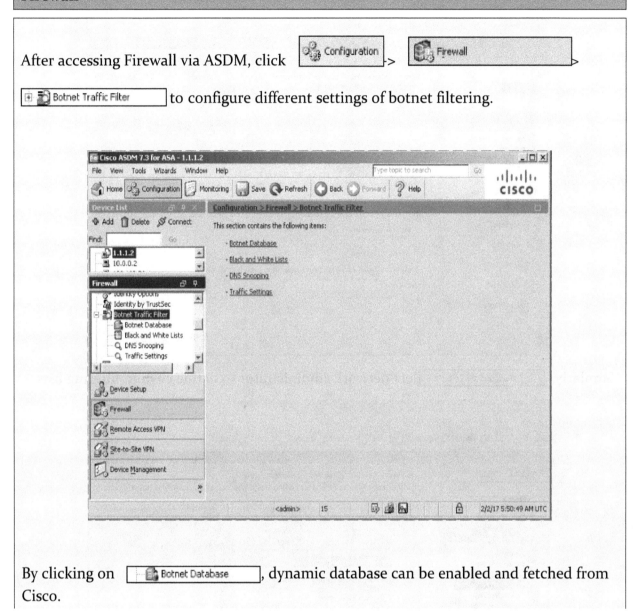

By clicking on [Botnet Database], dynamic database can be enabled and fetched from Cisco.

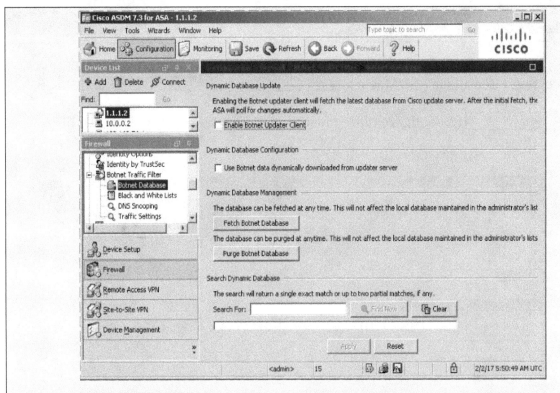

Similarly, Black and White Lists lets network administrator to define custom filtering lists.

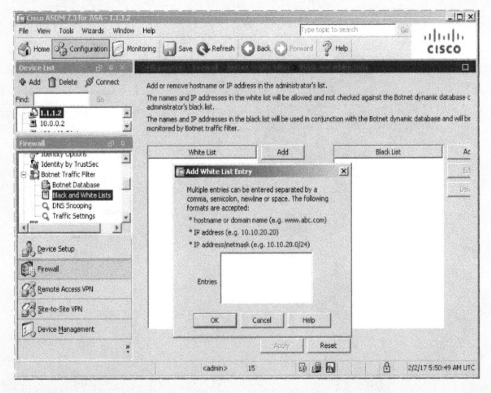

By clicking Traffic Settings , individual interface based policy can be applied.

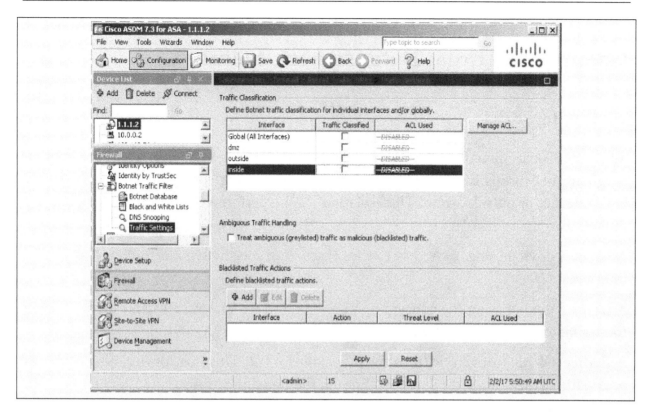

Chapter 04. Threat Defense Architecture

Technology Brief

The very primary function of using a dedicated device named as firewall at the edge of corporate network is isolation. Firewall prevents the direct connection of internal LAN with internet or outside world. This isolation can be performed in multiples way but not limited to:

A Layer 3 device using an Access List for restricting specific type of traffic on any of its interfaces.

A Layer 2 device using the concept of VLANs or Private VLANs (PVLAN) for separating the traffic of two or more networks.

A dedicated host device with software installed on it. This host device, also acting as proxy, filters the desired traffic while allowing the remaining traffic.

Although above features provide isolation in some sense, following are the few reasons a dedicated firewall appliance (either in hardware or software) is preferred in production environments:

Risks	Protection by Firewall
Access by Untrusted Entities	Firewalls try to categorize the network into different portions. One portion is considered as trusted portion like internal LAN. Public internet and interfaces connected to are considered as untrusted portion. Similarly, servers accessed by untrusted entities are places in special segment known as Demilitarized Zone (DMZ). By allowing only specific access of these servers, like port 90 of web server, firewall hides the functionality of network device, which makes it difficult for attackers to understand the physical topology of the network
Deep Packet Inspection and Protocols Exploitation	One of the coolest features of dedicated firewalls is their ability to inspect the traffic more than just IP and port level. By using digital certificates. Next Generation Firewalls available today can inspect traffic up to layer 7. Firewall can also limit the number of established as well as half-open TCP/UDP connections to mitigate DDoS attacks
Access Control	By implementing local AAA or by using ACS/ISE servers, firewall can permit traffic based on AAA policy

Antivirus and Protection from Infected Data	By integrating IPS/IDP modules with firewall, malicious data can be detected and filtered at the edge of network to protect the end-users

Table 18- Firewall Risk Mitigation Features

Although firewall provides great security features as discussed in Table 18, any misconfiguration or bad network design may result in serious consequences. Another important deciding factor of deploying firewall in current network design depends on whether current business objectives can bear the following limitations:

Misconfiguration and its Consequences: The primary function of firewall is to protect network infrastructure in a more elegant way than a traditional layer 3/2 devices. Depending on different vendors and their implementation techniques, many features need to be configured for a firewall to work properly. Some of these features may include Network Address Translation (NAT), Access-Lists (ACL), AAA base policies and so on. Misconfiguration of any of these features may result in leakage of digital assets, which may have financial impact on business. In short, complex devices such as firewall also require deep insight knowledge of equipment along with general approach of deployment.

Applications and Services Support: Most of the firewalls use different techniques to mitigate the advanced attacks. For example, NATing is one of the most commonly used feature in firewalls, and it is used to mitigate the reconnaissance attacks. In situations where network infrastructure is used to support custom-made applications, it may be required to re-write the whole application in order to properly work under new network changes.

Latency: Just as implementing NATing on a route adds some end-to-end delay, firewall along with heavy processing demanding features adds a noticeable delay over the network. Although high-end devices of Cisco Adaptive Security Appliance (ASA) series and other vendor's equipment have a very small throughput delay but some applications like Voice over IP (VoIP) may require special configuration to deal with it.

Positioning of Filtering Device in Network

The position of firewall varies in different design variants. In some designs, it is placed after the perimeter router of corporation while in some designs it is placed at the edge of the network. Irrelevant of its position, it is a good practice to implement the layered security in which some of the features like unicast reverse path forwarding, access-lists, etc. are enabled on perimeter routers. Features like deep packet inspection, digital

signatures are matched on the firewall. If everything looks good, the packet is allowed to hit the intended destination address.

Apart from acting as first line of defense, network layer firewalls are also deployed in within internal LAN segments for enhanced layered security and isolation.

Design and Deployment Considerations

Following are the industry best practices related to deployment of firewalls:

- Firewall should be the primary element in the overall security posture of network infrastructure
- Access policy that starts with "deny all" statement first followed by specific permit statements is recommended over "permit all" first and then explicit deny all statements
- It is recommended to place firewalls at the edge of network facing the untrusted network with respect to the organization
- Logging feature of firewall must be properly implemented. Many open source as well as specialized software are available to display Syslog messages and generate alerts for custom defined levels for forensic investigations
- Physical security, as well as access management of premises where firewall is deployed, must be ensured
- High availability must be ensured so that in case of one devices goes down, other takes its place, and overall business is not affected

Firewall Access Rules

A proper paperwork needs to done before moving to the configuration part of firewall. It helps in implementing the right policy for a given situation. Table 19 explains the different access policies, which can be implemented on firewalls:

Firewall Rule	Description
Services Based Access Rules	Rules are defined with respect to services, which will be accessed via firewall. An example would be to allow only HTTP/HTTPS traffic while denying everything else
IP Addressing Based Access Rules	These type of rules can permit or deny traffic based on source and destination IP address. An example would be to permit statement for IP address from inside or trusted network to the outside or untrusted network while denying everything else
Set of Rules Based on User Information	These kind of rules can integrate AAA services to define who can access specific services via firewall.

Table 19- Firewall Access Rules and their Descriptions

In Cisco firewalls, Access-list is the primary tool, which is used to match traffic for performing specific firewall feature. When applied on an interface either inbound or outbound, it is checked for more specific match from top to down fashion. If match is found, then proper action (permit or deny) is performed on packet. Due to presence of explicit deny, all statement at the end of ACL traffic is dropped if no match is found.

Regardless of which firewall access rules, defined above are used, following design considerations should be considered for implementing the access-list for above rules:

- Permit statements defined in access-list should be as specific as possible
- Users connected to internal or trusted interface should also be considered as part of overall security problem. Sometimes attacker use backdoors for generating attacks. Corporate user may be unaware of malicious activity being run by his/her computer and may also be allowed by firewall
- Unwanted network traffic should be filtered. For example, traffic coming from untrusted network with source address being one of the internal networks should be denied at the first place. Similarly, any packet with source address from RFC1918 or loopback address should also be filtered
- Logging feature should also be enabled and reviewed periodically to make sure its effectiveness
- As computer networks are designed to support certain business needs, balance should be maintained between functionality and security of business objectives

Similarly, in order to apply any changes on current policies defined on firewall, a procedural document or SOP should define at which states the changes are to be made, the need for it along with the authorized person who approves the changes. Following table summarizes the general rules in this regard:

Rule	Description
Redundant Rules	ACLs are always processed from top to bottom for more specific rules. If it is too long, a network administrator may add redundant entries for specific traffic. Although it does not create a security flaw, it makes Access list tedious and very difficult to understand
Shadow Rules	A shadowed rule exists because of incorrect order placement in the access-list, which may or may not have an impact on the current operation of infrastructure. If incorrect rule is placed above the correct one, current working sessions may be dropped because access-lists work from top to bottom fashion
Orphaned Rules	These rules contain incorrect IP addressing scheme either in source or destination address field. For example, if an IP address of 12.12.12.12/24 is never used on the inside network, then any statement with source address defined above will never be matched. Such statements only takes the space in configuration
Incorrectly Planned Rules	Such kind of rules exist because of miscommunication between business and technical teams. For example, if connection between client and server uses TCP port, 4141 and statement allows both TCP/UDP ports 4141, then such statements are considered as incorrectly planned
Incorrectly Implemented Rules	Such rules may result because of any kind of misconfiguration by network administrator due to lack of technical skills or any other reason. Examples include incorrect binding of port number or address etc.

Table 20- ACL Rules and their Descriptions

Cisco IOS Zone-Based Firewalls

IOS zone-based firewalls is a specific set of rules, which may help to mitigate mid-level security attacks in environments where security is also meant to be implemented via routers. In Zone-Based Firewalls (ZBF), interfaces of devices are placed to different unique zones like (inside, outside or DMZ) and then policies are applied on these zones. Naming conventions for zones must be easier to understand in order to be helpful at the hour of troubleshooting.

ZBFs also uses Stateful filtering, which means that if a rule is defined to permit originating traffic from one zone, say inside to another zone like DMZ, then return traffic would automatically be allowed. In order to allow originating traffic from both zones, two separate permit policies need to be applied.

One of the advantages of applying policies on zones instead of interfaces is that whenever new changes are required at interface level, then simply removing or adding interface in particular zone automatically applies policy on it.

ZBF may use the following feature set in its implementation:

- Stateful Inspection
- Packet Filtering
- URL Filtering
- Transparent Firewall
- Virtual Routing Forwarding (VRF)

Most of the features defined above are already explained in the previous sections. Virtual Routing Forwarding (VRF) are logical routing tables, used to divide the global routing table into multiple ones. Such features are useful in situations where one physical device is used to provide security feature to multiple clients. By creating virtual firewall for each client and VRF as a result of it, it makes troubleshooting as well as design a little bit cleaner as every client's configuration will be independent to each other.

Stateful Inspection

As the name depicts, it saves the state of current sessions in a table known as stateful database. Stateful inspection and firewalls using this technique normally deny any traffic between trusted and untrusted interfaces. Whenever an end-device from trusted interface wants to communicate with some destination address attached to untrusted interface of firewall, its entry will be made in the Stateful database table containing layer 3 and layer 2 information. Following table compares different features of Stateful inspection based firewalls.

Advantages	Disadvantages
Helps in filtering unexpected traffic	Unable to mitigate application layer attacks
Can be implemented on broad range of routers and firewalls	Except TCP, other protocols do not have well-defined state information to be used by firewall
Can help in mitigating Denial of Service (DDoS) attacks	Some applications may use more than one port for successful operation. Application architecture review may be needed in order to work after the deployment of Stateful inspection based firewall

Table 21- Advantages and Disadvantages of Stateful Inspection Based Firewalls

Consider an example of small office/home, where a limited number of users only require internet access. In this case, only two zones would be sufficient to implement the IOS zone-based firewall. Interface of router connecting to the internal LAN users can be placed in zone named, say "inside". Similarly, interfaces connected to public internet can be placed in another zone named as outside. In the second process, policies should be applied to permit traffic for required scenarios. For example, from inside to outside zone, HTTP/HTTPS traffic needs to be allowed.

Similarly, in case of corporate environment where multiple servers are meant to be accessed by outside world such as an ISP, which also provides hosting services to different clients, another zone needs to be created named as DMZ. Comparing this scenario with the small office/home, another policy would be needed to permit traffic from outside zone to DMZ zone.

Figure 24 shows the afore mentioned scenario:

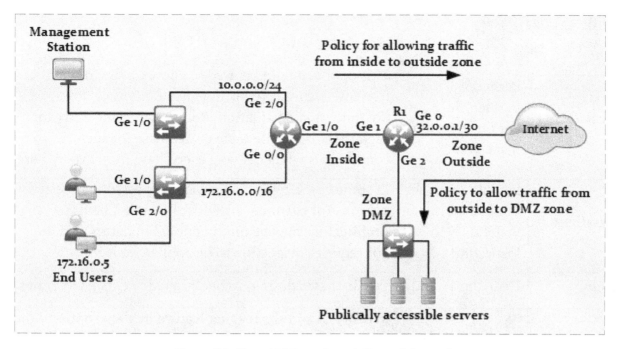

Figure 24- Cisco IOS Zone Based Firewall Scenario

Cisco Common Classification Policy Language (C3PL)

Cisco common classification policy language is the framework used to implement the IOS zone-based firewalls in Cisco devices. The steps involved are:

Class Maps: They are used to filter out the traffic that needs to be inspected. Traffic can be filtered by using information from Layer 3 up to Layer 7 of OSI model. ACL can also be referred in a class map for identifying traffic. Similarly, multiple match statements can also be used within single class map where every single match statement (a match-all condition) or even a single entry can be considered as a match (a match-any condition). By default, a class-map with name class-default is created in Cisco IOS, which can be used to match any kind of traffic hitting the device's interfaces.

Policy Maps: They are used to perform a specific kind of action on traffic matched by class maps. By referring a class-map, policy map can either inspect (Stateful inspection of traffic), permit (permit the traffic but no Stateful inspection), drop the traffic or generate log of it. A policy map is processed in top to bottom fashion just like ACL, and if multiple class maps are called within a single policy map, traffic would be matched until the match is found. If no class-map satisfies the traffic, then default action of implicit deny will be applied.

Table 22 summarizes the policy map actions:

Policy Map Action	Explanation	Application
Inspect	Permit the Traffic and Perform Stateful Inspection	This option should be used to allow traffic, initiated from users connected with trusted interface, towards the untrusted destination. Router will make entry for each session in state table or database for such connections while denying everything from everywhere
Pass/Permit	Permit the Traffic without Stateful Inspection	In some cases, reply traffic is not expected for initiated session. For example, a UDP Traffic in a Client/Server Architecture may be unidirectional in nature and does not requires inspection to be applied on it
Deny	Deny the Traffic	Traffic that is desired to be dropped between the zones
Log	Log the Traffic	In order to add the logging feature in above options, for example, to monitor the traffic dropped by policy map, this feature will also be used

Table 22- Policy Map Actions and their Applications

Service Policies: This command finally implements the policy, defined in policy-map applied on specific zone pairs. As from previous discussions, a zone-pair is just a unidirectional flow of traffic from one zone to another zone. For example, in Figure 24, two zone pairs need to be defined, one for inside to outside zone and second for traffic from outside to zone named as DMZ.

Without ZBFW configured, whenever a packet hits one of the interfaces of router, it will be matched for more specific entry in the routing table, which will eventually result in either forward or drop action. In case of ZBFW in place, Stateful database along with defined policy-map may also be checked before routing the packet to correct interface.

The Table 23 summarizes the action performed as traffic is intended to be moved between interfaces lying in different zones.

Ingress Interface Zone Membership	Egress Interface Zone Membership	Policy Definition on Zone Pair	Action
No	No	Does not matter	Forward the traffic
No	Yes	Does not matter	Drop the traffic
Yes (Zone X)	Yes (Zone X)	Does not matter	Forward the traffic
Yes (Zone X)	Yes (Zone B)	No	Drop the traffic
Yes (Zone X)	Yes (Zone B)	Yes	Policy is applied. Action of permit or deny will be applied as defined in the policy

Table 23- Service Policy Actions and their Applications

In short, implementing the ZBFW on Cisco's IOS involves the following steps:

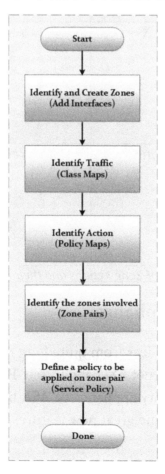

Figure 25- Steps involved in Implementing ZBFW

Self-Zone: Any kind of traffic directed towards the router itself is considered as a part of self-zone. For example, management traffic can be considered as part of self-zone. Similarly, traffic generated by router itself is also the part of self-zone. In Cisco devices, traffic to the self-zone either in ingress direction or in egress direction is permitted by default. However, filtering can be done on traffic directed towards the router by creating a zone pair (involving the self-zone) and applying policy to it. Contrary to named zones created for user traffic, if a zone pair involving self-zone is created, but no policy is applied on it, traffic will be permitted as summarized by Table 24

Originating Traffic Zone Membership	Destination Traffic Zone Membership	Policy Definition on Zone Pair	Action
Self Zone	Zone X	No	Forward the traffic
Zone X	Self	No	Forward the traffic
Self Zone	Zone X	Yes	Policy is applied. Action of permit or deny will be applied as defined in the policy
Zone X	Self Zone	Yes	Policy is applied. Action of permit or deny will be applied as defined in the policy

Table 24- Self-Zone Actions and their Applications

Cisco Adaptive Security Appliance

Cisco has been selling security devices from quite long time. Previous versions of firewalls were named as PIX (Private Internet eXchange), but PIX was replaced by new series of firewalls known as adaptive security appliance or ASA by 2005. ASA integrates the overall functionality of PIX along with some great new features.

ASA Series: Just as Cisco has created multiple series of routers and switches entertaining small office/home, enterprise networks up to the datacenters category, ASA also comes in different flavors as shown below:

Cisco ASA 5500 Series	Ideal for
Cisco ASA 5505-5515 Series	Small office Home office environment
Cisco ASA 5520-5545 Series	Medium sized offices
Cisco ASA 5550	Large enterprise environment
Cisco ASA 5585-X and Services Module	Data center / large enterprise networks
Cisco ASAv	Virtual ASA for virtual networking environment

Table 25- Cisco ASA Series

ASA features and services: Although ASA as a product provides many security features, it may be very difficult to highlight every single feature in this workbook. Following are the most prominent features of ASA firewalls:

- **Packet Filtering:** Simple packet filtering techniques like Access-Lists (ACL) can be used to perform traffic control by using layer 3 and layer 4 information. The main difference between ACL on a routers/switches and on ASA is the firewall uses subnet mask instead of wildcard mask as in routers and switches

- **Stateful Filtering:** By default, Stateful packet filtering is enabled on ASA, which means that firewall will keep track of every session initiated from trusted network to untrusted network. For example, a connection is made from client, say 10.0.0.2:800 to destination address, say 12.12.12.1:9090, assuming TCP socket connection is established. When the first packet from source hits the trusted interface of ASA, its entry will be made in Stateful database. The reply traffic of connection will only be allowed when source address and port number matches the saved state in the Stateful table

- **Inspection at Application Level:** In some cases, multiple ports pairs are used for over communication. For example, a client from inside zone trying to use FTP service. Now FTP uses port 21 for initial connection but uses port 20 for data transfer. If Stateful inspection is working, then the return traffic from data port, which is 20, will be dropped in return. By application inspection, ASA firewall learns dynamically about these ports and allows traffic from extra ports as well

- **NAT, DHCP, and IP Routing:** Cisco ASA firewalls also support multiple features of Layer 3 routing devices like NAT, DHCP and routing protocols like RIP, EIGRP and OSPF

- **Layer 3 and Layer 2 Operational Mode:** One way of ASA deployment is to assign IP address to different interfaces, and it will appear as an extra hop in end-to-end traffic path. This mode is known as *traditional* mode. Another case would be to deploy the firewall in *transparent* mode, in which no IP address is assigned to the interfaces of ASA, and it will act as multiport bridge with an ability to inspect the overall traffic just like traditional mode. The advantages of using the transparent mode is that end-users will be unaware of new additions in the network topology

- **VPN Support:** ASA can also be used to implement the Site-to-Site or SSL VPNs. The number of VPN connections ASA can make may depend on the purchased license

- **Mitigation against BOTNET:** A BOTNET is a group of infected computers, who can perform under a centralized command from an attacker. Most of the DDoS attacks are generated by BOTNETs. Cisco ASA can be configured to get regular updates related to BOTNET Traffic Filter Database from Cisco Systems Inc. in order to mitigate latest attacks

- **Advanced Malware Protection (AMP):** Cisco Next-Generation Firewalls (NGFW) provides the traditional firewalls feature along with some advanced malware protection features in a single device

- **AAA Support:** Just like routers and switches, authorization, authentication and accounting features can also be implemented either locally or in integration with some specialized hardware like Access Control Server (ACS)

- **ASA Security Levels:** Just like in ZBFW, where interfaces are placed in different zones, and then policy is applied on specific zone pair, ASA assigns different security levels to its interfaces. The basic function of security level is same as zones in ZBFW, i.e., to identify the trustworthiness associated with specific interface and end-devices connected to it. Higher the number assigned to an interface, the more trusted that interface would be considered. In general, Cisco ASA allows only 0-100 different security levels that seem enough for its operation

Consider an example of medium-sized corporate office where internal users must be entertained with secured internet access. Some of the corporate serves need to be accessed by public internet for business needs. In this case, three different security segments can be easily identified namely the *trusted* network and its users, which are connected to one of the interface of ASA. Secondly, the *untrusted* interface, which is the interface of ASA, connected to public internet. The third security segment would be the Demilitarized Zone (DMZ), where servers will be placed. With future amendments in

mind, three security levels need to be selected in such a way that it would not need to be reconfigured in case of any new network changes. As the highest security level that ASA can assign is 100, it would be assigned to the interface connected to LAN users. Similarity the most untrustworthy security level is 0, which will be assigned to interfaces connected to internet. 50 will be assumed as security level of DMZ so that wide range of security levels are still available for future scenarios.

In ASA, a name can also be assigned to an interface, for example, an interface with security level of 100 can be assigned a name of "inside". Same is the case for other networks. The following diagram summarizes the concept of security levels and their assignments.

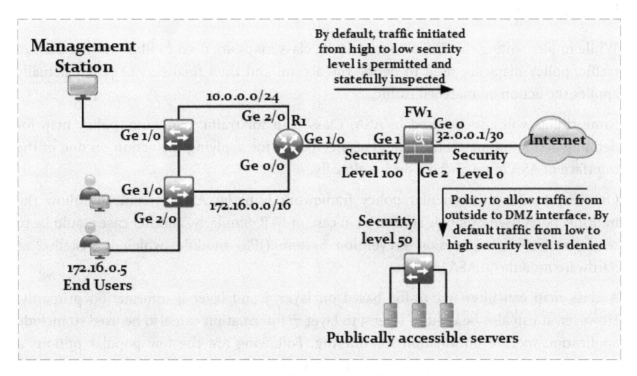

Figure 26- Cisco ASA Deployment in Production Environment

As Stateful inspection is enabled by default on Cisco ASA firewalls, traffic initiated from high-security level towards low-security level will be permitted. For example, traffic originated from security level 100 and 50 will be permitted towards security level 0 and return traffic as a result of it would also be allowed. However, traffic initiated from security level, say 50 to security level 100 would not be permitted by default. Access policy would be needed to allow traffic in this regard.

ASA Access Management: Just like routers and switches, both CLI and graphical methods can be used to access and manage the ASA firewall. Following are the official management techniques for accessing ASA firewall:

- **Command Line Interface (CLI):** With a little changes made, most feature and syntax for basic operation is same as Cisco IOS of routers and switches, etc.
- **ASA Security Device Manager (ASDM):** Just like Cisco Configuration Professional (CCP), which is used to manage routers via GUI, ASDM is used to manage ASA in the same way
- **Cisco Security Manager (CSM):** A GUI based tool, which can be used to manage the network devices like routers, switches and security devices like firewalls

Configure Default Cisco Modular Policy Framework (MPF)

While implementing the ZBFW in Cisco IOS, class maps are used to filter out the desired traffic, policy maps are used to define the action, and then final service policy actually applies the action on matched traffic.

Same things will also be used in ASA. Class map for traffic matching, policy map for defining action on match traffic and service policy for applying the action on one of the interface of ASA or on a whole device globally.

One way to use this modular policy framework is to let ASA dynamically allow the multiple ports used by single session as in case of FTP. Similarly, another case would be to send the traffic to Intrusion Prevention System (IPS) module, which is installed as hardware module on ASA chassis.

A class map can filter out traffic based on layer 3 and layer 4 information primarily. However, it can also be used to layer 5 to layer 7; information can also be used to include application-specific information for filtering. Following are the few popular options a class map can use for filtering specific traffic based on layer 3 and layer 4 information:

- Using Access-Lists (ACL)
- Using DSPC/IP precedence fields for prioritizing the traffic
- TCP/UDP port numbers
- VPN Tunnel groups

A policy map applies specific action on matched traffic by class-map, which may include:

- Transfer to IPS module
- Stateful inspection
- Prioritizing the traffic
- Limiting the rate of matched traffic

After defining the policy, it will be applied to an interface that has some security level. If policy is applied globally, it will be applied on all logical as well as physical interfaces of ASA device.

High Availability and Security Context: Just like First Hop Routing Protocols can be used on Cisco routers to provide load balancing and redundancy as well; two firewalls can be combined to provide similar results. In case one device goes down due to any software or hardware failure, second device will take its place. Two of the most common configurations of implementing high availability are Active/Standby failover and Active/Active failover. In Active/Standby failover, one device will act as primary firewall or active firewall while the second one will be in standby mode. Just like HSRP, the standard protocol traffic will be exchanged periodically between firewalls to check the status of active and standby firewalls. As shown in Figure 27, Ge 0/3 link will be used for the transmission of failover information. In case active firewall goes down, standby firewall will immediately take the charge.

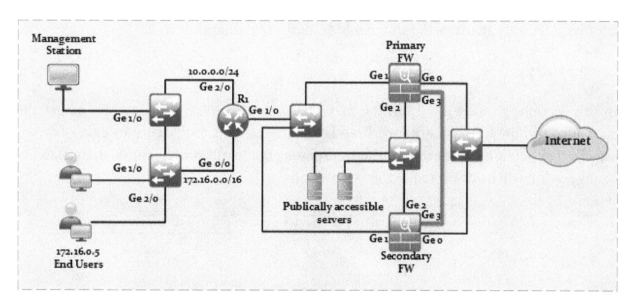

Figure 27- Cisco ASA Deployment in a High Availability Mode

High-end ASA devices allow making multiple virtual firewalls within the single hardware device. These virtual firewalls are known as *context*. Consider an example of a large service provider that also provides security features to its clients. Instead of using single hardware firewall for each client connection, service providers can use one high-end firewall and create multiple security contexts in it. In this way, each client will assume to have a separate piece of hardware as his or her next hop traffic will be isolated virtually within on hardware device. In, active/active failover, physical connection may remain

same as active/standby failover, so instead we make one firewall to act as primary for one context and second firewall to be primary for the second context just like HSRP can be tweaked to use multiple routers at the same time by making each router active for one unique VLAN.

Transparent and Routed Modes

By default, Cisco ASA works in layer 3 or routed mode in which an IP address is normally assigned to different interfaces of the device. End-hosts see firewall as a routing hop along the network path. In transparent mode, ASA works as layer 2 bridge and traffic flows through it without adding itself as routing hop between communicating peers. Consider it as a tap on a network, which is normally used to analyze the network traffic. In transparent mode, no IP address is assigned to an interface. However, name and security level is assigned to an interface to make it operational.

Just like Layer 2 switches and bridges, ASA in transparent mode also saves MAC address associated with an interface in its MAC address table. However, unlike conventional switches and bridges, which tend to broadcast the frame in case of unknown MAC address, ASA firewall drops the traffic if MAC address is unknown to it.

Case Study

In this section, a case study from the previous chapter will be used in order to get the clear idea of how to make a network design more resilient and secure in case of major attacks. Lab section will start with the transparent mode of firewall, and high availability configuration will be discussed in the last section.

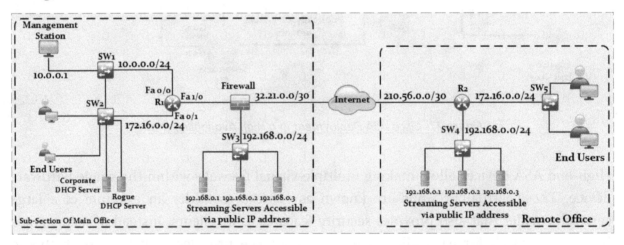

Figure 28- Threat Defense Architecture Case Study

Lab 4.1: Configuring Transparent Mode of Cisco ASA

As explained in theoretical section, transparent mode of Cisco ASA makes it a layer 2 device. No IP address is assigned to its interface. It means that IP address between firewall and internet in Figure 28 will be configured between R1 and internet in this lab. The only IP address assigned to Firewall in transparent mode is for management purposes just like in the case of L2 switches.

Firewall
FIREWALL(config)# firewall transparent

In case of the physical appliance, the above command will immediately restart the firewall. It is always advised to take a backup in case a rollback is required. After restart, the firewall will be in a transparent mode, which can also be checked with the following command.

Ciscoasa# show firewall

```
Firewall mode: Transparent
```

Now, assign the security level to different interfaces of ASA to make it operational.

Ciscoasa(config)# interface ethernet 0

Ciscoasa(config-if)# nameif inside1

```
INFO: Security level for "inside1" set to 0 by default.
```

Ciscoasa(config-if)# bridge-group 1

Ciscoasa(config-if)# security-level 100

Ciscoasa(config-if)# no shutdown

Ciscoasa(config)# interface ethernet 2

Ciscoasa(config-if)# nameif inside2

```
INFO: Security level for "outside1" set to 0 by default.
```

Ciscoasa(config-if)# bridge-group 1

Ciscoasa(config-if)# security-level 100

Ciscoasa(config-if)# no shutdown

Ciscoasa(config)# same-security-traffic permit inter-interface

The above command allows the flow of traffic between interfaces with the same security level.

Ciscoasa(config) # interface BVI 1

Ciscoasa(config-if) # IP address 32.21.0.3 255.255.255.0

32.21.0.3 acts as management IP address of ASA.

Verification

Trace the R2 IP address (210.56.0.2) from management station (10.0.0.1).

VPCS> trace 210.56.0.2

```
trace to 210.56.0.2, 8 hops max, press Ctrl+C to stop
 1   10.0.0.254          4.608 ms      11.724 ms     16.954 ms
 2   32.21.0.2           38.068 ms     29.874 ms     31.238 ms
 3   32.21.2.2           33.613 ms     29.430 ms     41.902 ms
 4  *210.56.0.2          49.690 ms     41.02 ms      43.9 ms
```

As it is clear from above trace result, firewall IP (32.21.03) is not appearing as IP HOP in traceroute result. The only reason from assigning IP address to BVI interface of ASA is for management purposes.

The following command can be used to current management IP address of ASA:

Ciscoasa# show IP address

```
Group : 1
Management System IP Address:
        IP address 32.21.0.3 255.255.255.0
Management Current IP Address:
        IP address 32.21.0.3 255.255.255.0
```

As firewall is acting as L2 device, MAC address table will also be formed, which can be checked with following command:

Ciscoasa# show mac-address-table

Interface	mac address	type	Age(min)	bridge-group
inside2	c20c.05a3.0000	dynamic	3	1
inside1	c206.fefd.0010	dynamic	3	1

Ciscoasa#

Lab 4.2: Configuring High Availability Feature of Cisco ASA

Cisco ASA firewall supports the physical hardware high availability feature, which means the secondary device will take place in case the primary device goes down due to any reason. Following are the few requirements of Cisco ASA high availability feature:

- Platform and hardware must be same.
- Mode of operation, i.e., transparent or routed mode should be same
- The license on both devices must be same

The following diagram shows the network topology being used in this lab.

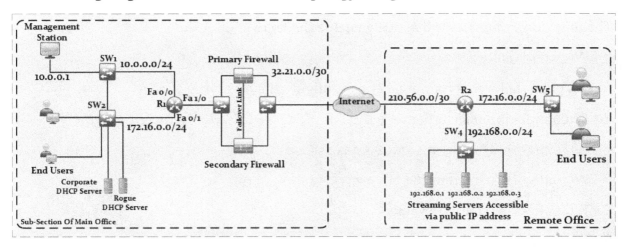

Figure 29- Configuring High Availability on Cisco ASA

As shown in Figure 29, there is *failover* link between both firewalls. There is a periodic exchange of messages between primary and secondary firewall. A configuration like IP addressing and security zone will be configured on the primary firewall. On the secondary firewall, there will be only high availability settings, and it will replicate the settings from the primary firewall.

Primary Firewall
First, change the hostname of Firewall.
Ciscoasa(config)# hostname P-FW
P-FW(config)#
The failover interface needs to be in UP state (even in case of no IP address on it)
P-FW(config)# interface ethernet 1
P-FW(config-if)# no shutdown
The following command will make P-FW as primary (active) device

P-FW(config)# failover lan unit primary

The following command will make Ethernet 1 as failover interface.

P-FW(config)# failover lan interface FAILOVER Ethernet1

INFO: Non-failover interface config is cleared on Ethernet1 and its sub-interfaces.

P-FW(config)# failover link FAILOVER Ethernet1

In the next step, an IP address needs to be assigned on failover interface.

P-FW(config)#failover interface IP FAILOVER 2.2.2.1 255.255.255.0 standby 2.2.2.2

The following command will actually enable the failover on ASA:

P-FW(config)#failover

At this point, failover is running. Let us configure the interfaces of ASA.

P-FW(config)# interface Ethernet 0

P-FW(config-if)# IP address 1.1.1.2 255.255.255.252

P-FW(config-if)# nameif inside

P-FW(config-if)# security-level 100

P-FW(config-if)# no shutdown

P-FW(config)# interface Ethernet 2

P-FW(config-if)# IP address 32.21.0.1 255.255.255.252

P-FW(config-if)# nameif outside

P-FW(config-if)# security-level 0

P-FW(config-if)# no shutdown

In the last step, ASA requires something (a parameter) to trigger the failover. The following commands make the interface as a trigger for failover. Whenever INSIDE or OUTSIDE interface fails, the secondary firewall becomes the active one.

P-FW(config)# monitor-interface inside

P-FW(config)# monitor-interface outside

That is all for Primary side configuration. Now, let us move to the secondary firewall for failover configuration. The secondary firewall is not configured. Only failover configuration will be done, and it will take the remaining configuration from the primary firewall.

Ciscoasa# configure terminal

Ciscoasa (config)# failover lan unit secondary

Ciscoasa (config)# failover lan interface FAILOVER Ethernet 1

INFO: Non-failover interface config is cleared on Ethernet1 and its sub-interfaces

Ciscoasa (config)# failover link FAILOVER Ethernet 1

Ciscoasa (config)# failover interface IP FAILOVER 2.2.2.1 255.255.255.0 standby 2.2.2.2

Ciscoasa (config)# failover

Once the Ethernet1 is UP with no shutdown command, the replication will take place. The most obvious proof will be the change of hostname of Secondary ASA.

Ciscoasa(config)# interface ethernet 2

Ciscoasa(config)# no shutdown

    Detected an Active mate

Beginning configuration replication from mate.

P-FW# End configuration replication from mate.

P-FW#

Show interface IP brief command on secondary ASA will not show the IP assignment on the interface as it is not in active state right now. However, show running-configuration the command can be used to see that entire configuration from Primary ASA has been replicated to Secondary ASA.

Verification

Show failover command can be used to verify basic failover configuration.

P-FW# show failover

```
Failover On

Failover unit Primary

Failover LAN Interface: FAILOVER Ethernet1 (up)

Unit Poll frequency 1 seconds, holdtime 15 seconds

Interface Poll frequency 5 seconds, holdtime 25 seconds

Interface Policy 1
```

```
Monitored Interfaces 2 of 60 maximum

Version: Ours 9.1(5)16, Mate 9.1(5)16

Last Failover at 16:07:08 UTC Feb 1 2017

        This host: Primary - Active

              Active time: 103 (sec)

                 Interface inside (1.1.1.2): Unknown (Waiting)

                 Interface outside (32.21.0.1): Unknown (Waiting)

        Other host: Secondary - Standby Ready

              Active time: 0 (sec)

                 Interface inside (0.0.0.0): Unknown (Waiting)

                 Interface outside (0.0.0.0): Unknown (Waiting)


Stateful Failover Logical Update Statistics

        Link : FAILOVER Ethernet1 (up)
```

Stateful Obj	xmit	xerr	rcv	rerr
General	14	0	13	0
sys cmd	13	0	13	0
up time	0	0	0	0
RPC services	0	0	0	0
TCP conn	0	0	0	0
UDP conn	0	0	0	0
ARP tbl	0	0	0	0
Xlate_Timeout	0	0	0	0
IPv6 ND tbl	0	0	0	0
VPN IKEv1 SA	0	0	0	0
VPN IKEv1 P2	0	0	0	0
VPN IKEv2 SA	0	0	0	0
VPN IKEv2 P2	0	0	0	0
VPN CTCP upd	0	0	0	0
VPN SDI upd	0	0	0	0
VPN DHCP upd	0	0	0	0
SIP Session	0	0	0	0
Route Session	0	0	0	0

```
    User-Identity          1         0          0          0

    CTS SGTNAME            0         0          0          0

    CTS PAC               0         0          0          0

    TrustSec-SXP          0         0          0          0

    IPv6 Route            0         0          0          0


    Logical Update Queue Information
                      Cur      Max      Total
    Recv Q:        0        17           13

    Xmit Q:        0        29           96
```

Similarly, the above command on secondary failover will show similar output but status will be secondary ready.

Secondary ASA

P-FW# sho failover

Failover On

Failover unit Secondary

Failover LAN Interface: FAILOVER Ethernet1 (up)

Unit Poll frequency 1 seconds, holdtime 15 seconds

Interface Poll frequency 5 seconds, holdtime 25 seconds

Interface Policy 1

Monitored Interfaces 2 of 60 maximum

Version: Ours 9.1(5)16, Mate 9.1(5)16

Last Failover at 15:55:45 UTC Feb 1 2017

       This host: Secondary - Standby Ready

          Active time: 0 (sec)

To test the failover feature, just right-click the Primary Firewall in lab and shut it down.

The following message will appear on secondary firewall after hold time pass out.

    Switching to Active

Again, use the show failover command to verify that secondary firewall has started acting as Active device.

P-FW# show failover | include This host

```
    This host: Secondary - Active
```

Lab 4.3: Creating Security Contexts in Cisco ASA

Cisco ASA lets network administrator to create multiple virtual firewalls (license dependent) known as security contexts. Following are the few scenarios where security contexts can help in making network security tasks easy:

- Large service provider, which is providing security, services to its clients. Instead of purchasing individual firewall for each client, different security context can serve the same purpose
- Administration of large or medium-sized enterprise environment with different departments. Creating different context for each department and then applying different security policies to each context can simplify the overall task
- There has been some network IP addressing overlapping in overall network topology and firewall services need to be provided overlapping network segments. To solve this problem, put overlapping segments in different security contexts

To demonstrate security context in this lab, two security contexts with name INSIDE and OUTSIDE will be created. INSIDE context will include Ethernet 0 interface. OUTSIDE context will include Ethernet1 and Ethernet 2. In this way, management and user's LAN will be isolated from other networks.

Firewall
By default, Cisco ASA comes in router mode and single context. It can be verified from following command:

FIREWALL(config)# show mode

```
Security context mode: single
```

To change its context mode from single to multiple, use the following command:

FIREWALL(config)# mode multiple

```
WARNING: This command will change the behavior of the device

WARNING: This command will initiate a Reboot

Proceed with change mode? [confirm]
```

A reboot will be required. Press "Enter" and firewall will restart to complete the operation. Once reboot is done, use the following command to verify:

FIREWALL# show mode

```
Security context mode: multiple
```

FIREWALL# show context

```
Context Name Class         Interfaces                      Mode    URL

*admin       default       Ethernet0, Ethernet1, Ethernet2 Routed  disk0:/admin.cfg

Total active Security Contexts: 1
```

By default, an admin context is created with everything being placed in it. To create INSIDE and OUTSIDE context and place interfaces in it, use the following commands:

FIREWALL(config)# context INSIDE

Creating context 'INSIDE'... Done. (2)

FIREWALL(config-ctx)# Description separate context for LAN

FIREWALL(config-ctx)# allocate-interface etherneto

FIREWALL(config-ctx)# config-url flash:INSIDE.cfg

FIREWALL(config-ctx)# exit

FIREWALL(config)# context OUTSIDE

Creating context 'OUTSIDE'... Done. (3)

FIREWALL(config-ctx)# description context for DMZ Servers

FIREWALL(config-ctx)# allocate-interface ethernet1

FIREWALL(config-ctx)# allocate-interface ethernet2

FIREWALL(config-ctx)# config-url flash:OUTSIDE.cfg

FIREWALL(config-ctx)# exit

Verification

To verify the above configuration, use the following command to see the created contexts and respective interfaces in each context:

```
FIREWALL# sho context
Context Name Class          Interfaces              Mode    URL
*admin        default        Ethernet0,Ethernet1,    Routed disk0:/admin.cfg
                             Ethernet2

 INSIDE       default        Ethernet0               Routed disk0:/INSIDE.cfg

 OUTSIDE      default        Ethernet1,Ethernet2     Routed disk0:/OUTSIDE.cfg


Total active Security Contexts: 3
```

From the above commands, it is clear that separate configuration files will be saved. The remaining configuration inside a specific context remains the same. To go into specific context for example OUTSIDE context, use the following command:

FIREWALL# changeto context OUTSIDE

FIREWALL/OUTSIDE#

FIREWALL/OUTSIDE# show interface IP brief

```
Interface    IP-Address      OK? Method Status    Protocol
Ethernet1    unassigned      YES unset  down      down
Ethernet2    unassigned      YES unset  down      down
```

FIREWALL/OUTSIDE#

As Ethernet1 and Ethernet2 were placed in OUTSIDE context, so above command shows only two interfaces.

Similarly, to perform different context like assigning IP addresses or IP routing, the commands are same. The ASA appliance will keep the information of different context like routing table and network traffic etc. separate from each other.

Chapter 5. Security Components and Considerations

Technology Brief

Virtualization and Cloud Security

Virtualization concept is taking major portion in current Data Center environments in order to reduce the administrative work and increase the flexibility and efficiency. For example, instead of using multiple servers, virtualized Virtual Machines (VMs) can be installed over a single high server by using software applications from different vendors like *VMWare, KVM, Xen,* etc. Cisco has also introduced different products in this regard such as Application Centric Infrastructure (ACI) ecosystem and Virtual ASA (ASAv). ACI provides centralized management and policy engine for physical, virtual, and cloud infrastructure. ASAv can be used to provide more granular control over applications running within virtual environment. By using virtualization, physical topology may vary from actual topology (running in virtual environment). Sometimes traffic may not leave physical environment, making virtual security solution to be preferred over physical firewall and security appliances.

Consider a Data Center environment with physical equipment as in Figure 30:

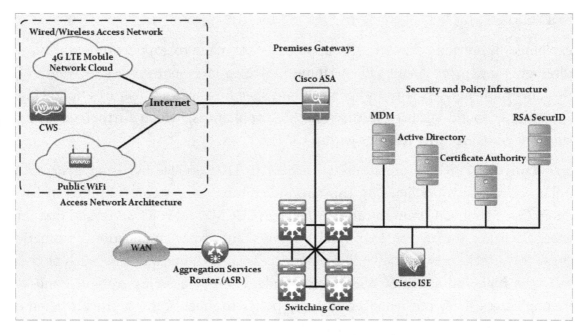

Figure 30- Data Center Network Topology

In case of virtualized environment, switching core or distribution layer may be based on Cisco Nexus 1000v switches, which are primarily designed to support server virtualization in a secure and transparent manner. In virtual switches, different VLANs can be created to separate different networks traffic at layer 2. In order to apply some restriction or filtration on different VMs connected to virtual switch, Cisco Virtual Security Gateway (VSG), a virtual appliance is used for it. After integration with Cisco Nexus switches 1000v, VSG not only provides trusted but also monitores within virtualized or cloud environment as per security policies.

Now on the top of secure switching segment, ASA is normally deployed as edge device facing the public internet, which is considered to as a non-secure. In case of cloud or virtualized environment, Cisco has another appliance called Cisco ASA 1000v Cloud Firewall, which can act as edge device for cloud-based environment supporting multiple IT services.

ASA Unified Communication Inspection Features

Cisco Unified Communications (UC) products help organizations to streamline their operations, maximize their employee productivity, enhance customer care and much more. As these products play critical role towards business objectives, Cisco has already integrated security features into its UC products and integrated them with Cisco ASA series firewall to enhance the overall security posture of network supporting voice and video solutions.

As explained in previous chapter, ASA appliances are made to support different business requirements, i.e., from Small Office Home Office to large enterprises as well as Data Center environments. Apart from licensing and specific hardware features, following are the commonly found security features in ASA appliances, which further enhance the already embedded security features within UC Products:

Access Control: Prevents unauthorized access to UC services by using dynamic and granular access control policies. In this specific context, access control refers to Layer 3 access to Cisco Unified Communication Manager (CUCM) and voice servers as first line of defense. Securing the access to physical servers and voice applications dramatically decrease the attacks possibility. Unlike older access control mechanisms, such as the use of ACL, the high-end series of ASA, for example, ASA 5500 series are voice and video aware appliances; They can inspect and apply policy to most of the protocols being used in today's voice/video communications for example SIP, H.323, SCCP and MGCP. ASA 5500 series can also track the voice connections and has some intelligent services such as voice protocol aware NAT that distinguishes latest ASA series from older platforms.

Threat Prevention: Built-in threat prevention systems help the systems from different types of attempts to exploit the overall infrastructure. The most common types of attack and exploits related to unified communication are Denial of Service (DoS), call eavesdropping, and user impersonation. Apart from protocol conformance and compliance checking, Cisco ASA series, especially 5500 series and above, can also use specific unified communication IPS signatures to detect and mitigate specific kind of attacks.

Network Security Policy Enforcement: Effective policy-making and administration support for users and applications. For example, calls can be permitted or denied from specific caller or domain. Specific applications can also be controlled, for example, denial of instant messaging over SIP, etc.

Encryption Services for Voice: Cisco Transport Layer Security (TLS) can be used for encrypting signals and media.

Support for Remote Users and Offices: Apart from SSL and IPSEC based VPN support, Cisco ASA also supports different features like phone proxy to securely extend the UC services to remote hosts, mobile and business-to-business communication scenarios.

In addition to the above features, different appliance of ASA has its own limitations for example maximum number of proxy sessions. To select the most suitable product for specific requirements, the datasheet along with licensing scheme must be kept in mind before purchase.

IPV6 Security Considerations

In order to secure the network segment either running on IPV4 or IPV6, it is a pre-requisite that network administrator has better understanding of that protocol. For example, a network administrator should know the basic terminologies of IPV6, configuration of different routing protocols like OSPF, EIGRP and most importantly BGP in IPV6. Only then, network administrators and engineers can identify the weak points within a protocol and apply suitable techniques for its protection.

As far as IPV6 is concerned, there is a category known as *First Hop Security*.

Neighbor Discovery Snooping (NDS)

NDS is used in local subnet to find out the neighboring machines. Therefore, the request will be in Neighbour Solicitation (NS) message, and response will be in Neighbour Advertisement (NA) message. Now to secure this process, NDS feature should be enabled, which builds a table to save the information regarding the ports and addresses involved in NS and NA processes.

Neighbor Discovery Inspection (NDI)

Just like Dynamic ARP inspection feature in IPV4 uses DHCP snooping table to make sure that nobody's else information is on network segment, NDI feature uses the information gathered by NDS feature to make sure that no one uses someone's else IPV6 information on local subnet.

RA Guard

One of the cool features of IPV6 is Stateless Address Configuration or SLAC. It works by using the Router Advertisement (RA) messages, which are sent periodically, although client, i.e., end-machines can also send Router Solicitation (RS) messages to ask for any router present in network segment. Therefore, after listening to RA messages, clients only need to decide the host ID of 128 bit IP address. In order to ensure that nobody on the same network is using the same host ID, Duplicate Address Detection (DAD) feature is used.

One problem in above automatic IP address assignment is that end RA message also contains the default gateway for client. Therefore, if someone else starts sending fraudulent RA messages on network segment, Man-in-the-Middle attack can result in a loss of critical information.

By using the RA Guard feature, a switch must be hard coded for what RA message should look like. So just like DHCP snooping feature, the non-authorized ports cannot advertise fraudulent RA messages on the network.

Secure Neighbor Discovery (SeND)

By using authentication in neighbor discovery process, rouge machine can be restricted from sending fake Neighbor Discovery (ND) messages on the network.

DHCPv6 Guard

Just like DHCP snooping feature in IPV4 protects clients from getting IP addressing from rogue DHCP server, DHCPv6 guard feature does the same in IPv6 environment.

IPV6 ACLs

One significant difference of IPV6 ACL from IPV4 ACL is that there is an implicit denial at the end of IPV4 ACL. However, most of the network administrators type explicit deny at the end of ACL to check the counters of denied traffic. In IPV6, there is also an implicit deny, but IPV6 ACL allows ND and NA traffic by default. Therefore, it should be kept in mind to explicitly allow ND and NA traffic before applying deny statement at the end of IPV6 ACL. To create IPV6 ACL and allow ND and NA messages use the following syntax:

Device-X (config) # ipv6 access-list <access-list-name>

Device-X (config-ipv6-acl) # permit icmp any any nd-na

Device-X (config-ipv6-acl) # permit icmp any any nd-ns

Security Components and Considerations MindMap

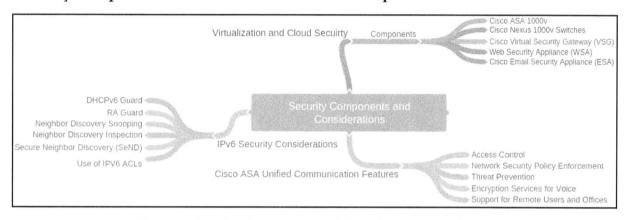

Figure 31- Security Components and Consideration's Mind Map

References

- http://www.Cisco.com/c/en/us/td/docs/wireless/prime_infrastructure/1-3/configuration/guide/pi_13_cg/ovr.pdf
- http://www.Cisco.com/c/en/us/products/security/security-manager/index.html
- http://www.Cisco.com/c/en/us/about/security-center/dnssec-best-practices.html
- https://tools.ietf.org/html/rfc793
- https://tools.ietf.org/html/rfc1180
- https://www.cisco.com/c/en/us/support/docs/ip/routing-information-protocol-rip/13769-5.html
- https://www.cisco.com/en/US/docs/internetworking/troubleshooting/guide/tr1907.html
- https://www.cisco.com/c/en/us/td/docs/ios-xml/ios/ipapp/configuration/15-mt/iap-15-mt-book/iap-tcp.html
- https://www.cisco.com/c/en/us/td/docs/voice_ip_comm/cucm/port/9_1_1/CUCM_BK_T2CA6EDE_00_tcp-port-usage-guide-91/CUCM_BK_T2CA6EDE_00_tcp-port-usage-guide-91_chapter_01.html
- https://www.cisco.com/c/en/us/td/docs/voice_ip_comm/cucmbe3k/8_6_2/system/cucmbe3k_862/04_port_list.html
- https://www.cisco.com/c/en/us/td/docs/voice_ip_comm/cucm/port/10_0_1/CUCM_BK_T537717B_00_tcp-port-usage-guide-100.html
- https://www.cisco.com/c/en/us/support/docs/ip/domain-name-system-dns/12683-dns-descript.html
- https://www.cisco.com/c/en/us/td/docs/ios-xml/ios/ipaddr_dns/configuration/15-mt/dns-15-mt-book/dns-config-dns.html
- https://www.cisco.com/c/en/us/td/docs/ios-xml/ios/ipaddr_dns/configuration/15-mt/dns-15-mt-book/dns-spl-dns.html
- https://www.cisco.com/c/en/us/td/docs/ios-xml/ios/ipaddr_arp/configuration/15-mt/arp-15-mt-book/arp-config-arp.html
- https://www.cisco.com/c/en/us/td/docs/ios-xml/ios/ipaddr_arp/configuration/15-mt/arp-15-mt-book.pdf
- https://learningnetwork.cisco.com/docs/DOC-23702
- https://www.cisco.com/c/en/us/td/docs/ios-xml/ios/ipaddr_arp/configuration/15-mt/arp-15-mt-book/arp-monitor-arp.html
- https://www.cisco.com/c/en/us/support/docs/ip/dynamic-address-allocation-resolution/13718-5.html
- https://www.cisco.com/c/en/us/td/docs/ios-xml/ios/ipaddr_arp/configuration/12-4/arp-12-4-book/arp-config-arp.html

- https://www.cisco.com/c/dam/en_us/about/ciscoitatwork/borderless_networks/docs/Cloud_Web_Security_IT_Methods.pdf
- https://www.cisco.com/c/en/us/products/security/cloud-web-security/eos-eol-notice-listing.html
- https://www.cisco.com/c/en/us/support/docs/security/cloud-web-security/200437-Cloud-Web-Security-Regional-Redirection.html
- https://tools.cisco.com/security/center/content/CiscoSecurityAdvisory/cisco-sa-20180711-wsa-xss
- https://www.cisco.com/c/en/us/td/docs/security/wsa/wsa11-0/user_guide/b_WSA_UserGuide/b_WSA_UserGuide_chapter_01100.html
- https://tools.cisco.com/security/center/content/CiscoSecurityAdvisory/cisco-sa-20180801-wsa-xss
- https://www.cisco.com/c/en/us/products/security/web-security-appliance/index.html
- https://www.cisco.com/c/en/us/support/security/web-security-appliance/tsd-products-support-series-home.html
- https://www.safaribooksonline.com/library/view/mike-meyers-comptia/9781260026559/
- https://www.safaribooksonline.com/library/view/comptia-security-all-in-one/9781260019292/
- https://www.safaribooksonline.com/library/view/comptia-security-review/9781118922903/
- https://msdn.microsoft.com/en-us/library/ff648641.aspx
- https://www.cisco.com/c/en/us/td/docs/ios/12_2/security/configuration/guide/fsecur_c/scfdenl.html
- https://www.ietf.org/rfc/rfc3704.txt
- http://www.cisco.com/c/en/us/td/docs/solutions/Enterprise/Campus/campover.html#wp737141
- http://www.cisco.com/web/services/downloads/smart-solutions-maximize-federal-capabilities-for-mission-success.pdf
- http://www.cisco.com/c/en/us/support/docs/availability/high-availability/15114-NMS-bestpractice.html
- http://www.ciscopress.com/articles/article.asp?p=2180210&seqNum=5
- http://www.cisco.com/c/en/us/td/docs/wireless/prime_infrastructure/1-3/configuration/guide/pi_13_cg/ovr.pdf
- http://www.cisco.com/c/en/us/products/security/security-manager/index.html
- http://www.cisco.com/c/en/us/about/security-center/dnssec-best-practices.html
- http://www.cisco.com/c/en/us/td/docs/ios-xml/ios/sec_usr_ssh/configuration/15-s/sec-usr-ssh-15-s-book/sec-secure-copy.html
- http://www.ciscopress.com/articles/article.asp?p=25477&seqNum=3
- http://www.cisco.com/c/en/us/products/security/ids-4215-sensor/index.html
- https://docs.microsoft.com/en-us/windows/desktop/memory/comparing-memory-allocation-methods
- https://docs.microsoft.com/en-us/windows/desktop/memory/virtual-address-space

- https://docs.microsoft.com/en-us/windows/desktop/memory/memory-pools
- https://docs.microsoft.com/en-us/windows/desktop/memory/memory-performance-information
- https://docs.microsoft.com/en-us/windows/desktop/memory/virtual-memory-functions
- https://docs.microsoft.com/en-us/windows/desktop/memory/allocating-virtual-memory
- https://docs.microsoft.com/en-us/windows/desktop/memory/heap-functions
- https://docs.microsoft.com/en-us/windows/desktop/memory/about-memory-management
- https://docs.microsoft.com/en-us/sysinternals/downloads/procmon
- https://docs.microsoft.com/en-us/sysinternals/downloads/pslist
- https://docs.microsoft.com/en-us/sysinternals/downloads/pskill
- https://docs.microsoft.com/en-us/sysinternals/downloads/process-explorer
- https://docs.microsoft.com/en-us/sysinternals/downloads/procmon
- https://docs.microsoft.com/en-us/sysinternals/downloads/procdump
- https://docs.microsoft.com/en-us/windows/desktop/memory/comparing-memory-allocation-methods
- https://www.safaribooksonline.com/library/view/mike-meyers-comptia/9781260026559/
- http://www.cisco.com/c/en/us/products/security/security-manager/index.html
- http://www.cisco.com/c/en/us/about/security-center/dnssec-best-practices.html
- http://www.cisco.com/c/en/us/td/docs/ios-xml/ios/sec_usr_ssh/configuration/15-s/sec-usr-ssh-15-s-book/sec-secure-copy.html
- http://www.ciscopress.com/articles/article.asp?p=25477&seqNum=3
- http://www.cisco.com/c/en/us/products/security/ids-4215-sensor/index.html

Acronyms

AAA	Bridge Protocol Data Unit (BPDU)	DDoS
Access Control Lists (ACL)	Cisco Certified Network Professional (CCNP)	DDoS attacks
Access Control Server (ACS)	Cisco Common Classification Policy Language (C3PL)	Denial of Service (DoS)
Access-Control Entries (ACE)	Cisco Configuration Professional (CCP)	DES
ACS/ISE Servers	Cisco Configuration Professional (CCP)	DHCP
Adaptive Security Appliance (ASA)	Cisco Discovery Protocol (CDP)	DNSSEC
Adaptive Security Appliance(ASA)	Cisco Discovery Protocol (CDP)	Domain Name System (DNS)
Adaptive Security Device Manager (ASDM)	Cisco IOS	DOS/DDOS
Adaptive Security Device Manager (ASDM)	Cisco Next-Generation Firewalls (NGFW)	Duplicate Address Detection (DAD)
Address Resolution Protocol (ARP)	Cisco Prime Infrastructure &	Dynamic Arp Inspection (DAI)
Advanced Malware Protection (AMP)	Cisco Prime Security Manager (PRSM)	Dynamic ARP Inspection (DAI)
APIPA	Cisco Security Manager (CSM)	EAP
Application Centric Infrastructure (ACI)	Cisco Security Manager (CSM)	EIGRP
ARP	Cisco Unified Communication Manager (CUCM)	Fully Qualified Domain Name (FQDN)
ASA Security Device Manager (ASDM)	Command Line Interface (CLI)	GIADDR
ASDM	Command Line Interface (CLI)	Health and Performance Monitoring (HPM)

Authorization, Authentication and Accounting AAA	Configuration Professional (CCP)	HSRP
BGP	Configure Default Cisco Modular Policy Framework (MPF)	Identity Services Engine (ISE)
Bits per second (BPS)	Content Addressable Memory (CAM)	Intrusion Prevention System (IPS)
AAA	Control and Provisioning of Wireless Access Points (CAPWAP)	IPS Device Manager (IDM)

IPS Manager Express(IME)	Role Based Access Control (RBAC)
IPS/IDP	Router Advertisement (RA)
ISP	Router Solicitation (RS)
Lightweight Access Point Protocol (LWAPP)	SCP
Link Layer Discovery (LLD)	Secure File Transfer Protocol (SFTP)
Link Layer Discovery Protocol (LLDP)	Secure Neighbor Discovery (SeND)
MAC	Simple Network Management Protocol (SNMP)
Management Information Base (MIB)	Spanning tree protocol (STP)
Man-in-the-Middle (MITM)	SSH
MD5	Stateless Address Configuration (SLAC)
Media Access Control Security (MACSec)	Top-Level Domain (TLD)
NAP (Network Access Protection)	Transport Layer Security (TLS)
Neighbor Advertisement (NA)	TTL
Neighbor Discovery Inspection (NDI)	Unified Communications (UC)
Neighbor Discovery Snooping (NDS)	Virtual ASA (ASAv)
Neighbor Solicitation (NS)	Virtual Machines (VMs)
Network Address Translation (NAT)	Virtual Routing Forwarding (VRF)
Network Address Translation (NAT)	Virtual Security Gateway (VSG)
Network Time Protocol (NTP)	VLAN
NTP	Voice over IP (VoIP)
On-Demand Routing (ODR)	Voice Over IP (VoIP)
OSPF,	Wireless LAN Controllers (WLC)
packets per second (PPS)	Wireless Services Modules (WiSMs)
PIX (Private Internet eXchange)	Zone-Based Firewalls (ZBF)
Port Address Translation or PAT	RADIUS
Private VLAN (PVLAN)	Resource Records (RRs)
Quality of Service (QoS)	

About Our Products

Other Network & Security related products from IPSpecialist LTD are:

- CCNA Routing & Switching Technology Workbook
- CCNA Security v2 Technology Workbook
- CCNA Service Provider Technology Workbook
- CCDA Technology Workbook
- CCDP Technology Workbook
- CCNP Route Technology Workbook
- CCNP Switch Technology Workbook
- CCNP Troubleshoot Technology Workbook
- CCNP Security SENSS Technology Workbook
- CCNP Security SITCS Technology Workbook
- CCNP Security SISAS Technology Workbook
- CompTIA Network+ Technology Workbook
- CompTIA Security+ v2 Technology Workbook
- Certified Information System Security Professional (CISSP) Technology Workbook
- CCNA CyberOps SECFND Technology Workbook
- Certified Block Chain Expert Technology Workbook
- Certified Cloud Security Professional (CCSP) Technology Workbook
- CompTIA Pentest+ Technology Workbook

Upcoming products are:

- CompTIA A+ Core 1 (220-1001) Technology Workbook
- CompTIA A+ Core 2 (220-1002) Technology Workbook
- CompTIA Cyber Security Analyst CySA+ Technology Workbook
- CompTIA Cloud+ Technology Workbook
- CompTIA Server+ Technology Workbook

www.ingramcontent.com/pod-product-compliance
Lightning Source LLC
Chambersburg PA
CBHW060135060326
40690CB00018B/3887